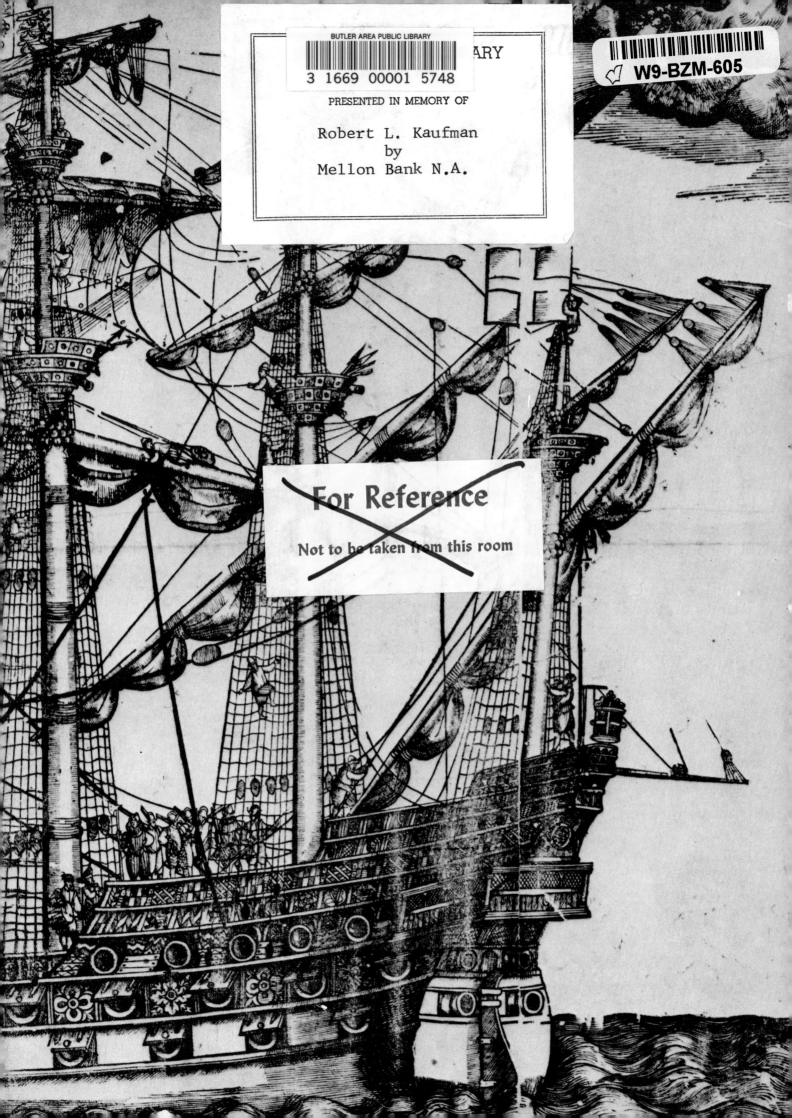

GREAT
BATTLE FLEETS

GREAT
BATTLE FLEETS

Oliver Warner

HAMLYN

London · New York · Sydney · Toronto

To Richard Simon

endpapers
A sixteenth-century woodcut of the English flagship
Ark Royal, not in fighting trim but decked out for
display.
British Museum.

title page
Howe's tactical victory over Villaret-Joyeuse on the
'Glorious' First of June, 1794, was the first fleet action
with the navy of France. By P J de Loutherbourg.
National Maritime Museum, Greenwich.

Published 1973 and
© Copyright 1973 by
The Hamlyn Publishing Group Limited
London · New York · Sydney · Toronto
Astronaut House, Feltham, Middlesex, England

Printed in Great Britain by
Jarrold & Sons Ltd, Norwich

ISBN 0 600 33913 0

Colour illustrations

Contents

INTRODUCTION

'Great Battle Fleets' – the very words summon up visions of floating might. This is exactly what they were, instruments to serve national ends and, in rarer cases, to help to ensure a more ordered world through the mere fact of their existence.

The question of prestige or honour also arose. To possess such a fleet has been all through history the result of huge and protracted effort on the part of thousands in and out of the naval service. To sustain it has required the expenditure of treasure, often grudged. Such an outlay has indeed more than once strained a country's resources beyond what could possibly be justified, and has led not to glory but to misfortune.

Battle fleets were in existence from very early times and in various parts of the world, but records of them are often meagre and imperfect. The accounts which follow describe the creation of such fleets since the sixteenth century. They indicate some of the uses to which they were put, they portray some of those who controlled them, they suggest the main reasons why they were dispersed.

It is probable that there will never again be fleets as big as those which sailed in the early part of this century. Sea power will continue to be exercised, but by means of the task force, the submarine, aircraft and missiles. Already, by the time the Second World War opened, fleets were numerically smaller than in the past. They had become fragmented in a way which would have seemed unorthodox to earlier generations. If this was partly due to cost, it was also because there could be no point in keeping a great fleet concentrated if the enemy did not possess one to challenge it. Later circumstances enlarged the scope of naval warfare because it was fought out in the Pacific on a scale which was unparalleled. Indeed the last great battle fleet, that of the United States of America, was the most powerful that ever went to war.

To the fleets were assigned some of the most impressive ships ever built. This was part of their attraction for the artists, who rose to the subject. What they recorded is for the most part a pageant of majesty and beauty but there was another and darker side, death and destruction, resulting from the use of the force with which the fleets were equipped. This too was graphically set down but, significantly, mainly from outside. The inboard hell of those ships of war in and after an encounter with the foe was a very different matter, and in any case difficult or impossible for the painter, or even for the camera, to convey. It was just as well. The grimmer side of a fleet's activities has to be remembered even when it is possible to enjoy with almost unalloyed pleasure what was intended to delight and to spread a sense of pride not only among those who served in the fleets but among those whose interests they guarded.

The histories of the fleets assembled in this book mingle or are linked. That is part of the fascination of the maritime story. The use to which ships of war are put is an ever varying business. It is one which, it seems, must develop for as long as nations, either through fear of attack or for reasons of pride, devote skill, energy, ingenuity and money to the construction of ever more remarkable creations.

In order to present a coherent narrative, fleets have been described in the order in which they made their most significant impact. Although they first appear at their zenith, it has seemed reasonable to give an indication of their origins and of their later development or dissolution. For instance the Spanish fleet with which the account opens played its part in history long after the sixteenth century, and its story needs to be continued at least in outline. Similarly the long gap between the fleet which foiled the Spanish Armada and the fleet which won at Trafalgar must be spanned, however briefly, if Nelson's tradition is to be understood.

An omission which may seem to call for explanation is that of the fleet of Portugal. The reason is that although this country's seamen were the cause of the development and extension of Western influence in Africa, the Far East and Brazil, she had been absorbed by Spain in 1580. When she regained independence, her fleet was no longer a considerable factor in the pattern of sea power. On the other hand, no apology should be necessary for including the Swedish fleet, for although its direct impact was not felt beyond European waters or far outside the Baltic, it was its very existence, in the eighteenth century, which brought about the creation of a rival maritime force by successive Russian sovereigns. This foreshadowed one of the more remarkable facts of the present day, a real or a possible Soviet presence almost everywhere a man-of-war can float.

opposite page
A Spanish print of the *Santissima Trinidada,* in her time the largest man-of-war afloat. She was captured by the British fleet at Trafalgar but sank before she reached Gibraltar. *Museo Naval, Madrid.*

7

THE SPANISH FLEET

When Philip II took control of the Spanish dominions from his father, the Emperor Charles V, it was at a time when the possibilities for expansion were almost limitless. The stranglehold of the Moors over the Iberian Peninsula had been broken after centuries of struggle, and Columbus, a Genoese in the service of Isabella of Castile, had in 1492 made the first of his voyages to the New World which would add fabulously rich territories to the Spanish crown. The Pope had given sanction to the division of the Americas, Africa and the Far East between Spain and Portugal, and the exploitation of his own great share was to be one of Philip's preoccupations.

Ships and men were his great necessities. He had to guard his dominions across the Atlantic. He possessed Flanders and the Low Countries, including modern Holland and Belgium, but they had to be sustained by sea. In the Mediterranean he needed a naval force to counter the depredations of the Moorish kingdoms of the northern shore of Africa. Still more menacing, because more powerful and better directed, there was the ever present threat of the Turks, who were expanding their conquests yearly. This was partly at the expense of Venice, but the lands of the Holy Roman Empire, with its centre at Vienna, were under constant attack. Unless the Turks were checked, traffic with the Near East, upon which Europe depended for so many commodities, could dwindle or vanish. The Mediterranean, around whose shores were some of the fairest lands of Christendom, was in dispute. Unless the principal nations of the south of Europe could unite and master the Turks by sea, the future looked grim.

Philip's naval experts were presented with two distinct requirements for sea war. Traditionally it was the galley, propelled by slaves, or those forced as punishment to man the oars, which was the dominant fighting vessel of the Middle Sea. This had been so since classical times, when fleets were commanded by soldiers, and tactics were employed which were designed to achieve victory by ramming and hand to hand encounters after boarding. Philip was well equipped in this respect, but oar power, even when supplemented by sail, as it usually was, did not suit the condi-

tions of the Atlantic or the often stormy route to the North Sea ports of the outlying Spanish possessions.

In the matter of sail, Philip could look to Portugal for enlightenment. That small country, ever since the time of Prince Henry the Navigator, had organised a series of increasingly adventurous voyages, which eventually compassed the entire coast of Africa and led to settlements in India and beyond. But Portugal had become too extended; her resources were strained. She would fall a prey to Philip during the course of his long reign – 1556 to 1598 – and he would take over not only her territories in Europe, Brazil, Africa and the Far East, but would have the advantage of the knowledge, won by experience on the broad oceans, of her navigators and shipwrights.

The first great service of the Spanish fleet, as an instrument of policy, was as part of the forces of the Holy Alliance. This had been formed largely by the patient diplomacy of Pope Pius V, whose aim was to unite the principal Christian powers against the Moslem incursion and to beat the Turks at sea. The most active members were Spain, which provided many of the finest ships, Venice, Genoa, Malta and the Papal States. Malta was then governed by the Knights Hospitallers of St John of Jerusalem, a militant order which, geographically and in every other respect, was at the heart of resistance to the enemy. The island, which had been granted to the Knights by the Emperor Charles V in 1530, had sustained a great siege in 1565. Had it then fallen, it is possible that the Pope's efforts would have been in vain, for the enemy would have possessed an island fortress which, as far more recent events have shown, could become the key to Mediterranean strategy.

An immediate crisis had arisen because in March 1570 Venice had refused an ultimatum from the Sultan demanding the surrender of Cyprus. Appeals for help were made to Spain as well as to the Pope, and within a year the Holy League, which for some years had been more of an aspiration than a reality, had taken shape and been given urgency. This came too late to save Cyprus and its defenders, who were barbarously

Philip II of Spain
(reigned 1556–1598), a
portrait by the Venetian
master, Titian, showing
the King when young.
Prado, Madrid.

An engraving celebrating the part taken by Pope Pius V in forming the victorious Alliance which succeeded at Lepanto. *National Maritime Museum, Greenwich.*

as the Gulf of Corinth. He decided to concentrate his forces, which he believed would outnumber the Christians.

There were, in fact, some 300 Allied ships assembled off Sicily, after Don John, with the Spanish squadrons, arrived on 25 August 1571. The admiral's flagship, according to contemporary representations, had a fore and a mainmast, lateen rigged, as was usual in the Mediterranean, and thirty-two oars each side. She had been built three years earlier for the Viceroy of Catalonia. The leading artists of Barcelona had painted the after-castle. The hull was highly decorated, and there was a lion's head carved at the tip of the long beak.

The fleet was formed into five squadrons, each of different nationalities, but it was soon found that, owing to disparity in numbers, it would be desirable to mingle them to some degree. There were seven fast galleys in the van when the ships left harbour on 16 September. These were in the charge of Juan de Cardona, who flew a green pennant. The main body, with Don John and the *Reale* in the centre, had the Papal galleys on the right wing, and Venetians on the left. Beyond the Papal ships, on the extreme right wing, were the Knights of Malta, and on the extreme left were more Venetians, commanded by Agostino Barbarigo, who flew a yellow pennant. Santa Cruz with the reserve brought up the rear. The Venetians were short-handed, and Spaniards were drafted into some of their ships to make good the numbers. This, and bad weather off Sicily, had led to delay and to quarrelling among Allies highly charged with national pride.

Six Venetian galleasses were included in the galley fleet, which was provisioned and supplied by miscellaneous ships under sail, proceeding independently. The galleass, heavily gunned, was an attempt to combine the manoeuvrability of the galley with the fire power and the seakeeping characteristics of the galleon. The idea was, when battle was joined, that the galleasses should attack first, two abreast, softening up the enemy with their artillery before the galleys dashed in to ram and board.

Owing to continued bad weather, with head winds which made the rowers' work even harder than usual, the Allies took ten days to reach Corfu. There they heard rumours of disaster at Cyprus, and these were confirmed a few days later. They also heard of local devastation from the hands of Ulick Ali, an Algerian corsair, once a Calabrian fisherman, who had thrown in his lot with the Turks. It was now the turn of Don John to send out a reconnaissance, and the resulting report was encouraging. It was thought, erroneously, that Ali Pasha had at most only some 200 vessels at his disposal, and it was also believed that there was plague among the Turks, reducing their available manpower.

Ali Pasha now called for a second report from his own scouts. The Allied fleet was counted when off Corfu, but darkness prevented the

executed before the opposing fleets had met: but the action of the Turks, who had promised to spare the lives of the Venetians, added to the ferocity with which the campaign was conducted.

At this time the race of admirals scarcely existed. Grandees, with military experience, were appointed to command fleets. Rank was necessary, to ensure obedience and respect. Martial skill was either there already, or it was taken for granted. The Allied leader, blessed by the Pope, and with his flagship, the *Reale*, embellished with Christian banners and sacred emblems for what was to be in the nature of a crusade, was Don John of Austria. This young man of twenty-five was a natural son of the Emperor Charles V, and thus a half-brother of King Philip. He had served with distinction on land, and was to show himself an inspiring leader afloat. At the head of the purely Spanish contingent was the Marquis of Santa Cruz. Other notables were Prince Antonio Colonna, commanding the ships of the Papal States; Andrea Doria of Genoa; Giustiniani, Grand Master of the Knights of Malta; and Sebastiano Veniero, at the head of a Venetian force based partly on Crete and partly on Corfu.

The Allied rendezvous was to be at Messina, which left the Adriatic open for an attack on Venice: but the Turks let the chance slip, preferring to spread terror and desolation along the coast of Greece. One of their captains, however, hoisting black sails at night in order to proceed unseen, made a swift reconnaissance to discover the Allied strength, and returned to Ali Pasha, the Moslem commander, to report. Ali was at that time anchored in the Gulf of Lepanto, now known

reconnoitring captain from seeing the whole of Don John's force, and he too returned with an optimistic estimate of its size. In view of the intelligence they had received, both commanders-in-chief sought battle at once, since both believed themselves to possess numerical superiority. Both moved towards the mouth of the Gulf of Corinth.

But the Christians still had bad weather to contend with, and their fleet spent four days at anchor under the lee of the island of Cephalonia. Then, on 6 October, matters improved. That night, Don John anchored off the mainland at Cursolari, barely twenty miles from the Moslems, at the entrance to the Gulf of Corinth. At first light on 7 October, men in the leading galleys sighted Turkish sails. Don John put a Roman pilot ashore to climb a small headland and count their numbers. He brought back news that there were some 250 enemy vessels assembled, nearly fifty more than Don John had available. As it was too late to draw back, the admiral, hoping much from the galleasses, which were a new element in sea warfare and were already in the van, gave the order to advance.

Behind the galleasses came 150 galleys in line abreast, with the rest in reserve under Santa

left
The Marquis of Santa Cruz, who commanded the Spanish reserve at Lepanto and would have led the Armada of 1588 but for his untimely death. *Museo Naval, Madrid.*

below
An allegorical print at the Arsenal in Venice showing the first clash of the fleets at Lepanto.

Detail of the mêlée
between the Christian
and Moslem galleys at
Lepanto, showing
the destruction of a
Moslem flagship.
*National Maritime
Museum, Greenwich.*

Cruz. Don John had given orders for the wings to approach inshore as close as possible, to avoid being outflanked. The leader himself went among the ships in a fast galley, standing at the prow and holding a crucifix on high. He was cheered by the crews, and when he returned to the *Reale* he ordered a gun to be fired as a signal that action could begin when the enemy came within range. A standard was then broken at the mainmast, portraying Christ crucified, with St Peter and St Paul on either side.

Ali Pasha's standard was white, with verses from the Koran inscribed on it in gold letters. At first he had the wind astern of him, and he was bearing down fast when it suddenly dropped. Oars then became the sole motive power for both sides. Ali had promised the Christian slaves at his rowing benches their freedom if he won the battle. 'If the day is yours,' he added, 'then God has given it you.'

At about midday the galleasses of the centre and the left, gunners at their pieces and musketeers in the fighting-tops, began to open fire. The Turks had nothing to match them, and great confusion was caused in the oncoming lines of ships. Shot smashed the long sweeps and caused heavy casualties among the oarsmen. Nevertheless the Moslems came on dauntlessly, and at first with considerable success. Barbarigo took the first shock of attack, and to add to his difficulties some of the enemy managed to slip inshore, as Don John had feared they might, and were able to take the Venetians in the rear. Janissaries, the picked men of the Turkish fleet, fought like demons. They boarded Barbarigo's own galley, clearing the deck as far as the mainmast. Barbarigo himself was killed by an arrow. Twice his galley was captured. Twice it was retaken in fierce counter-attacks. In one of these Mahomed Sirocco, leader in the original advance and renowned for his intrepidity, was thrown into the water and his galley captured. He was rescued by the Christians only to be instantly beheaded and his remains thrown back into the sea. This incident had a marked effect on the nearest Turks, most of whom then proceeded either to beach their ships or to withdraw up the Gulf, leaving the Christian left victorious.

In the centre and on the right, the day was long in doubt. Ali Pasha, as was the custom in all sea battles whenever circumstances allowed, made straight for the enemy flagship, withholding his fire as long as he could. When it was opened, the mainmast of the *Reale* was almost fractured by a cannon ball and an entire bench of rowers was mown down. Then the galleys crashed into each

right
Three sea commanders:
Andrea Doria of Genoa
(left), Santa Cruz of Spain
(centre) and Luis
Requesens of Spain
(right).
*Duchess of Santo Mauro,
Madrid.*

opposite page
A print by a member of the
Bruegel family showing a
galleon under sail and an
oared galley fitted with a
lateen sail.
*National Maritime
Museum, Greenwich.*

15

other, splintering their long beaks, and allowing that close fighting in which the Spaniards excelled.

Twice they boarded Ali Pasha's ship, and twice they were repulsed. It was then the turn of the Janissaries, who got a foothold on the *Reale* and began to gain ground on decks slippery with blood. Don John led a counter-attack in person, but his ship was in some danger of capture until Colonna came up in support. He boarded the Turkish flagship by the stern, and caught at a disadvantage by fresh ships, the Turks were quickly overwhelmed.

Ali Pasha, wounded in the head by an arquebus, tried to buy his life with a promise of treasure. It was in vain. A Spaniard cut him down, hacked off his head, and took it to Don John. The admiral ordered it to be thrown into the sea, but he was disobeyed. The soldier concerned mounted it on a pike, which was held aloft on the prow of the captured flagship, while the Ottoman standard, inscribed with the name of Allah 29,000 times, was lowered from the main-top. Consternation reigned among all the Turks who saw it, for this sacred emblem had never before been taken in battle, even momentarily.

The left and centre victorious, all should have been well; but it was not so on the right. Andrea Doria and Ulick Ali had spent valuable time trying to outflank each other, until Ulick himself suddenly made off towards the centre with some of the best of his ships. There ten galleys made a concentrated attack on the Knights of Malta. Giustiniani was killed, and his standard fell into enemy hands. This was a moment of great triumph for the Turks, but it did not last. Santa Cruz appeared with the reserve, and Andrea Doria moved across to the threatened squadron. Ulick Ali managed to fight his way clear, and, helped by a following wind, he made off with what remained of his ships through the Straits of Ithaca. He was pursued, but in insufficient strength. A number of Ulick's galleys doubled back and fought a bloody engagement with Cardona, whose men suffered terribly before help arrived.

This was a last setback in a victory otherwise wonderfully complete. Nearly 30,000 Turks are believed to have been killed, and the larger number of their galleys were sunk, beached, or towed away by the Christians. 12,000 slaves who had served unwillingly in Ali Pasha's fleet were released, and in the evening, with the wreck-littered sea whipped up by a south-east wind, Don John led his weary men to more sheltered waters where he sent off two fast galleys to Messina with the news of his triumph.

The event was commemorated throughout Europe by artists and craftsmen of every sort; rightly so, for it was one of the most decisive sea

right
One of a set of English playing-cards showing the Duke of Medina Sidonia, who commanded the Armada of 1588, and Admiral Recalde. *National Maritime Museum, Greenwich.*

below
A falconet or light gun of the period of the Armada. The weight was about 400 lbs and the ball about 1¼ lbs. *Museo del Ejercito, Madrid.*

Knave

Don Alphonso Duke of Medina, Cheife Comander of ỹ Spanish Fleete. & John Martin Recalde, a great Seaman.

battles on record, and had a profound effect in checking the Moslem incursion. And as men of all principal Italian states, as well as those of Spain and Malta, had taken part, there was no lack of virtuosity and splendour in celebration, as many examples in churches and elsewhere testify to this day.

One of the humbler participants was Cervantes, later to gain immortality as the author of *Don Quixote*. He had been a volunteer serving under Andrea Doria, and his experience was grim, for his ship the *Marquesa* was at one time hard pressed. Cervantes had been ill with fever before the battle, but he had risen from his sick bed and fought valiantly. He was wounded in his left hand, of which he never again had the full use.

Lepanto was the finest hour in the history of the Spanish navy. Spain had the honour of providing the Christian leader, and the skilful handling of the reserve, under Santa Cruz, ensured the outcome of the battle. Don John had been too fiercely engaged personally, at the crisis, to direct where the reserve strength should be applied. This had been left to the initiative of the reserve commander, and he had not failed.

Don John did not long survive the battle, and it would have been to Santa Cruz that Philip II would have looked as leader of the next important campaign in which his navy was to be engaged. This became known as the Enterprise of England. It was an example of mismanagement all the more difficult to understand from Philip's point of view, since he had no excuse for misreading the temper and quality of the people he was about to engage. Moreover Philip, earlier in life, had been married to Mary Tudor and had actually lived in England.

But he was a man of fixed ideas. His word was law, and no one was able to correct his misconceptions. His preparations went forward relentlessly, with the aim of invading and subduing England, and thus ensuring her return to the Catholic faith, of which he was a paramount champion. Pope Pius V had pronounced Queen Elizabeth a heretic, and had absolved her subjects from their allegiance. Philip believed, in spite of his own knowledge of her, and of the fact that Elizabeth had reigned since 1558 with exceptional skill, that the mass of her nation would at best be half-hearted in their efforts to repel him.

He was never more mistaken, as he should have learnt from the trouble his representatives were having in countering revolt in the Netherlands. This had broken out in 1572, the year after Lepanto, under the leadership of William the Silent, Prince of Orange and Stadholder. William had been murdered at Delft after an heroic resistance lasting twelve years, and Philip believed— again wrongly—that his rebellious subjects would be brought to their knees by the Duke of Parma, who commanded the best infantry in Europe.

The strategic plan was a sweep up the Channel from Philip's Atlantic ports by an Armada which would be joined off the Flemish coast by a fleet under Parma. The whole would consist of over 550 ships of various kinds, ranging from galleons to barges, and nearly 100,000 men. This was a far greater force, numerically, than England could ever hope to muster, and it seemed clear to Philip that his fleet could dominate the Thames estuary and thereafter seize London.

A letter from Philip II to the Duke of Medina Sidonia dated February 1588. The last lines are in the King's own hand. *National Maritime Museum, Greenwich.*

There was no secret about Spanish intentions, which were known throughout Europe and in particular to the Dutch, who as Protestants were England's friends. But even with the huge resources at his command, for Philip to assemble, equip and man a fleet of the size proposed the most elaborate preparations were needed. These could be disrupted by raids in force, as Drake proved when he descended upon Cadiz in 1587 and by consummate tactics and effrontery did so much damage that the invasion was delayed by a year, during the course of which Santa Cruz died. He was replaced by the Duke of Medina Sidonia, an amateur at sea, and, as it proved, a most unfortunate choice.

The force which set out from Lisbon in the summer of 1588 was formidable enough, though far less so than had originally been planned. It was made up of some 130 ships and about 30,000 men. There were 65 galleons or great ships, 25 *urcas* or store ships, 32 smaller ships, 4 galleasses and 4 galleys. The men fell into four distinct classes: 8,000 sailors, 2,000 rowers, 19,000 soldiers and 1,500 volunteers and non-combatants. The latter included a quota of priests, who are not considered lucky afloat.

The Duke's flagship was the *San Martin,* which carried 117 sailors and 300 soldiers. The principal commanders, some of them veterans of Lepanto, were Flores de Valdes, who had charge of the Castilian squadron which, with the Portuguese under Medina Sidonia's direct command, were in the van, a compliment to their prowess; then, well protected, came the *urcas* all together under Juan Gomez de Medina, followed by a Biscayan squadron under Juan Martinez de Recalde, Andalusians under Pedro de Valdes, Guipuscoans under Miguel de Oquendo, and Levanters under Martin de Bertendona. The galleasses were Neapolitan and, as at Lepanto, they went ahead.

The Duke of Parma, by Otto van Veen. The Duke commanded the Spanish army in the Low Countries at the time of the Armada.
Musées Royaux des Beaux-Arts de Belgique, Brussels.

They were in the charge of Hugo de Moncada but, like the handful of galleys, they were not a success.

The course of events, from the Spanish point of view, was one of gallant but complete failure. At first the Armada met with bad weather and at one stage had to turn back. Once in Channel waters, which were reached by 19 July, there was excellent discipline. This was sustained, except for some confusion arising from a series of mishaps to individual ships, for well over a week. Medina Sidonia was harassed indeed by a number of attacks, carried out at long range by experienced seamen in well-found ships with reasonably efficient guns, defending their Queen and their homeland in an area of sea with which they were all familiar. Yet when the Spaniards anchored in Calais Roads on 27 July, their officers may have been gloomy, but their fleet was largely intact. If Medina Sidonia could get news from Parma, all

might still be well: but Parma was at Bruges, and sternly occupied by the Dutch.

In fact, the crisis came off Calais, on the night of 28 July, when Lord Howard of Effingham, the English Commander-in-Chief, sent down eight fire-ships with the wind and tide. Panic followed. Guns shotted, sails set, rudders fixed and crews removed, these fearsome vessels came 'spurting fire, and their ordnance shooting, which was a horror to see'. The contemporary who wrote these words did so with reason. In days of sail fire at sea, especially by night, had a peculiar terror.

Within minutes, cables were cut; hulls and rigging were damaged in frequent collisions as the Spaniards tried to make their way as best they could for what they hoped was the safety of the open sea. Even so, one fine ship, the galleass *San Lorenzo,* drove so hard on to Calais Beach that she was immovable. Howard attacked her, and de Moncada was killed in the assault, the

An engraving by John Pine purporting to show the capture of the galleon *Rosario* by Drake in the Armada fight, with a surround of English commanders. *National Maritime Museum, Greenwich.*

A painting by Vroom, whose signature is on the flag of a Dutch ship attacking Spanish galleys off the Flemish coast, 1617.
Rijksmuseum, Amsterdam.

only Spanish commander of high rank to fall in action, though Pedro de Valdes, whose flagship had been damaged earlier through collision, became the prisoner of Sir Francis Drake. The careful discipline and order which Medina Sidonia had achieved until then was gone for ever. Even the wind seemed to have turned against King Philip.

By the dawn of 29 July, the Armada was in complete disarray. The ships were strung out along the coast between Gravelines and Dunkirk, and from their base at Flushing the Dutch rebels could frustrate any attempt by the Spaniards to gain the shelter of Antwerp.

The wind seemed about to force them on to a lee shore, while the tireless English, short of ammunition and stores, but as waspish and audacious as ever, gave them no respite. 'We have them before us,' wrote Drake, 'and mind with the Grace of God to wrestle a fall with them.' Wrestle he did, but the fickle elements changed in Spanish favour, the wind backing from West-North-West to West-South-West. Although half a dozen wrecks were left behind on the banks of Zeeland, to make plunder for the Dutch, Medina Sidonia was able to make for home as best he could round the north of Scotland.

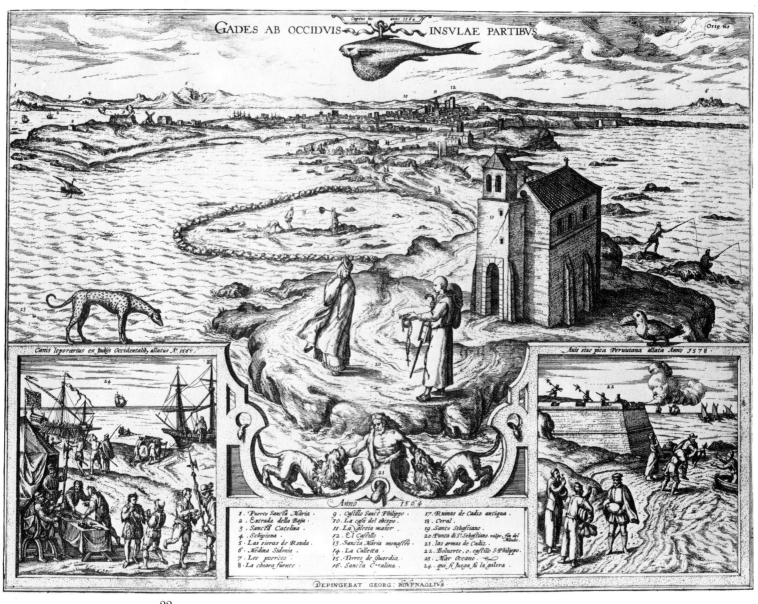

Schau, Portugal, dein Häupt, die Tochter des Ulissen
die grosse Kaussmans-stadt, Lisbone, klein gerissen
auss dieses kleine blat, schau ihren weiten bau
in dieser äng' albier; und wiltu mehr; so schau
ihr eignes wesen an, und lenke dich vom schatten
zum lichte selbst, das ist Europe komt zu statten,
mit seinem milden blitz, Dan hier ist alles feil,
was köstlichs haben mag der Erden bestes theil.

Si de mon fondateur la renommeé est mort,
Qu' importe: antiquité annoblit mon berceau;
Mes palaix, que l'amour jusques aux nues porte,
Monstrent, en ce pourtrait du monde le plus beau,
L' Amerique par mer dedans mes havres glisse
L' Indien baraué se recree en mon port,
Mais je ne vis jamais ancrer cher moy Ulisse
Tais toy Rome, mon heur de sept montaignes fort.

Wie heut Ulisses voor de stichter van dit wonder!
Hy sach nooit achter zich Gibraltar op de togt.
Wat is 't indien mijn wieg verschuilt in d'eeuwen onder;
Daar ick den Tagus kus in goud verrykte vegt.
Hier komt America op Suiker rieden reysen
Hier dobbert d'Indiaan geroost door 't ooster licht.
By seven bergen zich verheffen mijn Palleysen
Zints ken ick Rome niet voor s'werelds hooft gesicht.

Clemendt de Ionghe excudit.

opposite, top
A view of Cartagena in 1786, showing details of this Mediterranean naval base and its fortifications. *Palacio Real, Madrid.*

opposite, bottom
A painting by Samuel Scott of Anson's capture of the Spanish treasure galleon *Nuestra Senora de Covadonga* (right) in 1743 during his voyage of circumnavigation (1740–1744). *National Maritime Museum, Greenwich.*

left
Don John of Austria, Philip II's half-brother, who led the Christians to victory at Lepanto in 1571. *Prado, Madrid.*

right
A painting by Hendrik
Cornelius Vroom of a
fight between Spanish
ships and Barbary
corsairs, 1615.
*National Maritime
Museum, Greenwich.*

below
Design for a tapestry
celebrating the defeat of
the Armada.
*National Maritime
Museum, Greenwich.*

During that weary circuit he was beset by storms and suffered terrible shortages. Many ships and crews perished, most of them on the Irish coast. The total loss was 63 out of the force which had set out, crusade-like, from Lisbon. It was very nearly one half.

'I sent my ships to fight against the English, not the winds and waves,' wrote Philip sadly. Elizabeth's subjects sang in jubilation in St Paul's Cathedral, and echoes of their triumphal chorus were heard in Holland, whose seamen had done more than a little to cause it.

If the Armada was an instance of anticlimax on an extended scale, so was much of the rest of Spanish naval history. There were no more Lepantos; only a series of protracted defensive campaigns and actions against English, Dutch and French, sometimes singly, sometimes in combination. Spain had so much territory that she was vulnerable in every quarter, and although she was able to draw wealth from overseas, it seemed to help her little. For she rarely produced sovereigns or statesmen of calibre, and although often drawn into coalitions and alliances, her record at sea was dismal. She could build fine ships, 'Spanish beauties' the English used to call them, and her men were brave and indeed chivalrous in war. But able leadership at sea was beyond her capacity.

Piecemeal, Spain's possessions were prised from her grasp. The Dutch and English inherited what Portugal had won in the Far East and Spain had failed to keep. Dutch, English and French shared the spoils of the Caribbean, which Spain had looked upon as her own.

Early in the nineteenth century the South American countries achieved their independence, under cover of British sea power and often with the active help of British naval volunteers. By the end of the century only Cuba and Puerto Rico, the Philippines, some other scattered islands, and parts of Africa were left of the great empire which had owed allegiance to Philip II. It was then that Spain, which had assembled the first great battle fleet, succumbed to the power of the United States, which was to create the last. This was the final occasion when Spain looked to sea power to protect her interests, and, because she had learnt so little all through the centuries, it failed her hopelessly.

In 1898, with the Cubans in the full tide of revolt against their Spanish overlords, the United States warship *Maine* was sent to the island to safeguard American citizens. An explosion, of which the cause was never fully established, resulted in the complete loss of the man-of-war and 260 of her crew. A Commission of Enquiry did not exclude the possibility that the disaster had been due to an exterior cause, and the Americans accused the Spanish of exploding a mine under the vessel. With what seemed to some to be precipitate haste, yet with overwhelming popular backing, the American government declared war on 25 April.

left
The decorated stern of a model of the ship of the line *Real Carlos*, built in 1787.
Museo Naval, Madrid.

below
A graceful model of a Spanish 74-gun ship built at Cartagena towards the end of the eighteenth century.
Museo Maritimo, Barcelona.

It was apparent that matters would be decided at sea. The United States fleet was then comparatively weak, but matters of strategy were decided with commendable speed. This was not surprising since Captain Alfred Thayer Mahan, an officer whose writings on sea power were to have a profound influence on world affairs, who had studied its effects more shrewdly than anyone else then living, and who already had held the post of Director of the Naval War College, was appointed to the War Board.

The Atlantic squadron was at once reinforced, while on the Spanish side Admiral Pasquale Cervera, who had been sent from Cadiz with orders to destroy the American naval base at Key West in the event of hostilities, rightly judged that with no well-appointed base in the West Indies available to him, his mission was impossible. He made for the Cape Verde Islands instead, there to wait upon events.

American success came first in the Pacific. There, Commodore George Dewey, who had trained a small force of four cruisers and two gunboats to a high state of efficiency, steamed to Luzon in the Philippines, and continued down the coast towards Manila. He found Don Patricio Montojo at anchor there, and with his ships in no state to fight at sea. Shortly after dawn on 1 May 1898 Dewey attacked and destroyed the entire opposing force. He scored 171 hits on the Spanish ships, while only 17 answering shots reached their target. The Spaniards suffered the loss of 381 killed and wounded. The American total was 7 wounded.

The story was repeated in the Atlantic. Admiral Cervera sailed in due course from the Cape Verde Islands to the Caribbean, refuelled at Curaçao by leave of the Dutch, and made for Santiago, on the south coast of Cuba. There he was destroyed, after a running fight during which the Spaniards showed themselves totally unfit to meet the conditions of modern war. An American military force was landed, and soon captured the city. Another took the island of Puerto Rico with insolent ease. Not a single reverse had occurred for the United States, and within the space of a few weeks Spain had lost both her navy and the control of islands she had consistently mismanaged: for the people of the Philippines were as fiercely in revolt as the Cubans.

The long-term effect of this, the last external war in which the Spanish navy was engaged, was unexpected. The condition of Cuba was such that it was necessary to establish an American protectorate. And at the peace treaty the United States acquired the Philippines, the Pacific island of Guam and Puerto Rico, while the taking over of the Hawaiian Islands was hastened by the events which had recently taken place.

The failure of the Spanish navy had thrust the United States into a process of expansion to which its people had given no thought, and for which they were unprepared. If the course of a war is unpredictable, so are its consequences.

THE ELIZABETHAN FLEET

In the Prologue to the third Act of Shakespeare's *Henry V* there is an evocative passage describing the sailing of a battle fleet from Southampton, carrying an expedition on the King's business overseas.

*Play with your fancies, and in them behold
Upon the hempen tackle ship-boys climbing;
Hear the shrill whistle which doth order give
To sounds confused; behold the threaden sails,
Borne with the invisible and creeping wind,
Draw the huge bottoms through the furrow'd sea,
Breasting the lofty surge: O do but think
You stand upon the rivage and behold
A city on th'inconstant waters dancing;
For so appears this fleet majestical....*

Shakespeare may have seen the Elizabethan fleet with his own eyes, yet he was speaking of a time well before his own, and it is fitting to remember it, for the forces which defeated the Spanish Armada were no new creation. England had raised fleets for centuries, and the men of the Cinque Ports, originally Hastings, Dover, Sandwich, Romney and Hythe, later extended to include Rye and Winchelsea, flew a flag on which were emblazoned significant emblems. One of them was half lion, half ship. This was a peculiar instance of heraldic ingenuity but, as so often, it was appropriate.

Henry V himself had ordered the building of a great vessel, the remains of which still exist in the Hamble River. Later sovereigns, in particular Henry VII, who built a dry dock at Portsmouth, had been very much aware of the need for an efficient naval force. Henry VIII, in the final year of his long reign, established a properly organised naval administration. It endures to this day, modified and transformed to meet the needs of a very different age.

Henry was as concerned with sea affairs as any of his predecessors had been. In 1514 he caused a ship to be built, the *Henry Grâce à Dieu* or *Great Harry,* which was originally fitted with 184 guns, many of them light. Although impressive to look at, she was not a success until she was rebuilt, on a smaller scale, in 1539. She was burnt in 1545. An artillery expert, Anthony Anthony, made a drawing of her which shows her like a medieval floating castle. She would have seemed antique and cumbersome in Elizabeth's time.

The King created by Letters Patent a body of Commissioners, each responsible for a specific department, under the general guidance of the Lord Admiral, who was one of the great Officers of State. Henry did not live to see this body at work, and until the Spanish crisis it dealt mainly with routine. By then, the Commissioners were functioning reasonably well, though the number of royal ships they had to regulate was not large. There were only 34 in operation against the Armada. The rest of the fleet, 197 ships in all, was made up of armed merchantmen, many of them equipped by the City of London, and of squadrons from the Cinque Ports and elsewhere. Some were very small indeed.

The Lord Admiral's flagship was the *Ark* or *Ark Royal.* She had originally been called *Ark Raleigh* but her builder, Sir Walter Raleigh, handed her over to the Queen without payment, although long afterwards £5,000 was remitted from a debt he owed her. Drake's flagship, as Vice Admiral, was the *Revenge,* which when commanded by Sir Richard Grenville was later sunk after an epic fight with a Spanish squadron off the Azores. These were ships. They were not primarily transports for troops, as were so many of those of Spain. Indeed the total English manpower involved was not much more than 15,000, half that of their enemies.

The principal leaders, both ashore and afloat, were highly professional men, most of them with varied experience at sea. Some, like Drake, the first English circumnavigator, became legends in their own lifetime. Among the more outstanding was Sir John Hawkins, who commanded the *Victory,* the first of her name in an illustrious succession of men-of-war. Hawkins was knighted during the course of the running fight with the Spanish, and no one deserved the honour more. Drake had once been his pupil and subordinate. Later, Hawkins became one of the Navy Board Commissioners, and in 1577 was chosen as Treasurer of Marine Causes. He was in great part responsible for the building of the newer of the Queen's ships, and they were to show themselves the best fighting vessels afloat.

Another notable officer at sea, alas, antipathetic to Drake, was Martin Frobisher, who was knighted by Lord Howard on Elizabeth's behalf at the same time as Hawkins, and with the enemy not far distant. Ashore, men of the calibre of Raleigh and Grenville looked after matters of defence. Raleigh understood the Lord Admiral's tactical problems perfectly. Years later, when the Queen was dead and he was languishing in prison under her successor, Raleigh embarked on a *Historie of the World*. In this ambitious book there appeared a passage on 'The Art of War at Sea' which proves the matter up to the hilt.

The Spaniard, he wrote, *had an army aboard them, and he* [Howard] *had none: they had more ships than he had of higher building and charging; so that, had he entangled himself with those great and powerful vessels, he had greatly endangered this Kingdome of England. For twenty men upon the defences are equal to an hundred that board and enter. But our Admiral knew his advantage, and held it: which had he not done, he had not been worthy to have held his head.*

Raleigh went on to speak about sea fighting in general terms, and his remarks accurately describe the method used by Howard during the run up the Channel.

I say that a fleet of twenty ships, all good sailors, and good ships, have the advantage, on the open sea, of an hundred as good ships, and of slower sailing. For if the fleet of an hundred sail keep themselves near together, in a gross squadron, the twenty ships, charging them upon any angle, shall force them to give ground, and to fall back upon their own next fellows; of which so many as entangle, are made unserviceable, or lost. Force them they may easily, because the twenty ships, which give themselves scope, after they have given one broad side of artillery, by clapping into the wind, and staying, they may give them the other, and so the twentie ships batter them in pieces with a perpetual volley, whereas those, that fight in a troup, have no room to turn . . . .

Medina Sidonia's rigid discipline was essential to control his fleet, but it was also a hampering factor. Raleigh and the admirals were keenly aware of this.

The Queen was also equal to the high occasion. She rode among her troops at Tilbury. Few in numbers though they were, in spirit they were as stout as any living. Elizabeth was in her middle fifties, and she had reigned over them a long time, but she was still, for the common man, romance personified. James Ashe, an indifferent poet but a true-hearted liege subject, wrote in *Elizabetha Triumphans*:

A page from the Victualling Accounts of Edward Bashe, Surveyor, dated 1558.
National Maritime Museum, Greenwich.

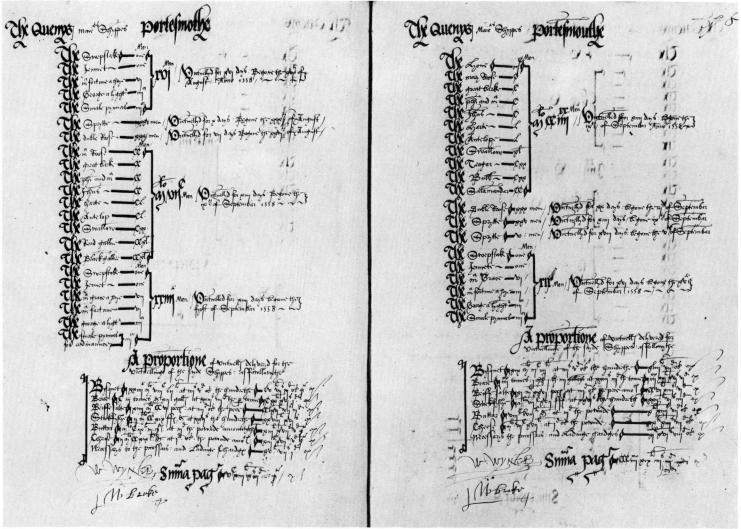

Her stateliness was so with love-show joined,
As all there then did jointly love and fear.
They joyed in that they see their Ruler's love:
But feared lest that in aught they should offend
Against herself, the Goddess of the Land.

It was in this atmosphere that the Queen made her famous Tilbury speech. It could not have been actually heard by many, such was the wind, but those who caught her words spread them, and they are thus remembered. She told her soldiers that she had not come among them for 'recreation and disport', but to lead them in person:

... being resolved, in the midst and heat of the
battle, to live or die amongst you all, to lay down
for my God, and for my Kingdom, and for my
people, my honour and my blood, even in the dust,
I know I have the body of a weak and feeble
woman, but I have the heart and stomach of a
king, and of a king of England too, and think foul
scorn that Parma or Spain, or any prince of
Europe should dare to invade the borders of my
realm; to which, rather than any dishonour
shall grow by me, I will myself take up arms, I
myself will be your General, judge and rewarder
of every one of your virtues in the field. I know
already for your forwardness you have deserved
rewards and crowns, and we do assure you, in
the word of a prince, they shall be duly paid you.

These were just the words for the time, and although 'rewards and crowns' were never to be more than metaphorical, the sense was plain, and the Queen was cheered to the echo.

But at the time, it was ships above all that mattered. The Queen's subjects had shown that they could make ships fit to sail round the world. They also made some of the world's best guns, a skill they shared with the Swedes. The industrial areas of the time were forest lands, particularly those with iron in the soil. The raw material of the Elizabethan and later fleets was found mainly in the woods of the southern counties, as was much of the iron for the guns.

Spain, in a last-minute search for as many heavy cannon as she could assemble, equipped herself partly from England, the pieces reaching her circuitously. Indeed, such was the demand for the products of the Weald of Kent and Sussex, of Hampshire and the Forest of Dean – timber for shipbuilding, which absorbed huge numbers of mature trees, and wood to make charcoal for the forges which produced the guns, that a time would come when there would be a serious shortage. Once an age of maritime expansion had begun, there could never be too much good oak. The best timber took a century and more to become of practical use to the shipwright.

In the era of sail, it was uncommon for ships of the higher rates to be sunk by gunfire alone.

A modern sculpture by Sir W Reynolds-Stephens, 'A Royal Game', showing Elizabeth I and Philip II moving ships as on a chessboard.
Tate Gallery, London.

Lord Howard of Effingham (1536–1624), who led the English fleet against the Armada. Daniel Mytens shows him in old age.
National Maritime Museum, Greenwich (Greenwich Hospital Collection).

Certainly no vessel of any size belonging to Philip's Armada was thus lost. The casualties occurred from internal explosion, as in the case of the galleon *San Salvadore,* or collision, as with Pedro de Valdes's *Nuestra Senora del Rosario,* or as the result of the mere appearance of fireships. Storm, fog and navigational error claimed further victims. Both sides expended an enormous quantity of powder and shot, so much so that the Spaniards used up most of their reserves and the English, though they could replenish from nearby bases, were not by the end of the chase in any better position. Sound and fury, signifying little, was the upshot of the cannonading. Sickness, failures in victualling, shortages of every sort were the real reasons why the pursuit was not more effective.

The English, all through the centuries of sail, used their guns with a different purpose from most of their opponents, especially the Spaniards and the French. They liked to fire on the downward roll of the ship, with the aim of damaging hulls, setting the splinters flying among the crews, and thus demoralising them. The alternative, firing on the upward roll, was intended to injure rigging, spars and sails, crippling the enemy ship. At the battle of 1588, both methods were ineffective, though both were tried.

As regards the relative size of the vessels engaged, chroniclers were long confused by the loose way in which the word 'tonnage' had come to be used. This was understandable because from very early times the size of a ship was measured by the amount of wine in jar, cask, ton or butt that she could hold. Had the containers been standardised, all would have been simpler, but while in England the butt held 126 gallons of liquor, in Spain it held much less, and in Venice it differed again. So the ton came to mean something different in the various countries with a regular merchant marine. It is for this reason that when accounts state that the Duke of Medina Sidonia's *San Martin* was of such and such a tonnage, while the *Ark Royal* was far less, it is rash to jump to conclusions. They were probably about the same size.

Six years before the Armada, a certain Matthew Baker was instructed to devise a satisfactory way of measuring ships. He was a good choice and was probably suggested by Hawkins. It had been the custom of Henry VIII to reward good craftsmen with a life pension, which was really a retaining fee so that the King could call upon the services of the recipient whenever he needed him. One of the earliest of such 'pensioners' was James Baker, Matthew's father, who in 1537 was given fourpence a day from the Treasury. He won renown as a builder of ships of war, and the art of mounting heavy guns inboard is said to owe much to his skill. His son was the first to be called Master Shipwright, and his knowledge was of the greatest help to the Queen in the strenuous years during which her fleet was preparing.

Choosing a vessel called the *Ascension* of London, Matthew Baker found she could carry 320 butts of Bordeaux wine in her hold. As two butts went to a ton, the *Ascension* was of 160 tons burden, that is to say, she could carry such a burden or load. Baker then measured the ship and found she was 54 feet on the keel, was 24 feet broad inside the plank, while her depth in hold was 12 feet. Multiplying these figures gave him 15,552. He then looked for a divisor which would give him the 160 he required. This was found to be $97\frac{1}{5}$ though for reasons of simplicity Baker seems to have made the divisor 100 in his promulgated 'Rule of Tonnage'. To obtain the ship's 'dead weight', or total for purposes of register, he thought fit to add one third to the 'burden'.

During the reign of Charles I, the shipwrights of the Thames were to claim that 'Mr Baker's old way' was to divide by 94; and further, that he always measured outside the plank, for breadth, and to the bottom of the keel, for depth. If this claim were conceded, it would have made a ship appear to be 20 tons larger in every 100. As the shipwrights were paid by the ton when they sold ships to the King, their memories of Mr Baker were much to their own advantage. But in this particular case, Charles had good advisers. It *pleased* them to remember that 'Mr Baker's old way', established in Queen Elizabeth's time, and

Sir John Hawkins (1532–1595), when aged 44. He was Treasurer of the Navy, and was knighted for his part in the defeat of the Armada. *National Maritime Museum, Greenwich.*

never questioned in that of King James, was, 'Length of the keel (leaving out the falsepost); the greatest Breadth within the plank; the Depth, from that breadth, to the upper edge of keel—multiplying these together, and dividing by one hundred.' The King had the last word.

In the matter of ships and in other ways, Philip learned something from his defeat of 1588, as has often been the way with the losing side at sea. He strengthened his defences overseas to such a degree that Drake's later forays did not repeat the success of those of his earlier career. But the ships of what was known as the Indian Guard had an active enough life convoying the treasure sent to Spain, and sometimes there were resounding captures. Only four years after the Armada,

Sir John Burgh in the ship *Roebuck* took the richest single prize of the age. This was the *Madre de Dios* or *Great Carrack*. She was a tall-sailed, high-sided, rather cumbersome vessel, built mainly for cargo carrying. Burgh took her after a chase of sixteen hours, and experts reckoned that her value was not less than £500,000, a sum which needs to be multiplied many times to gain some idea of a modern equivalent. Such hauls continued from time to time, perhaps the most famous being the capture of a galleon sailing from Acapulco to Manila by Commodore Anson in 1743. This made Anson's fame and fortune towards the end of a war-conditioned circumnavigation which in romantic flavour was almost the equal of Drake's.

A map showing the progress of the Armada up-Channel, harassed from the west by the English. Engraved by A Ryther, 1590. *National Maritime Museum, Greenwich.*

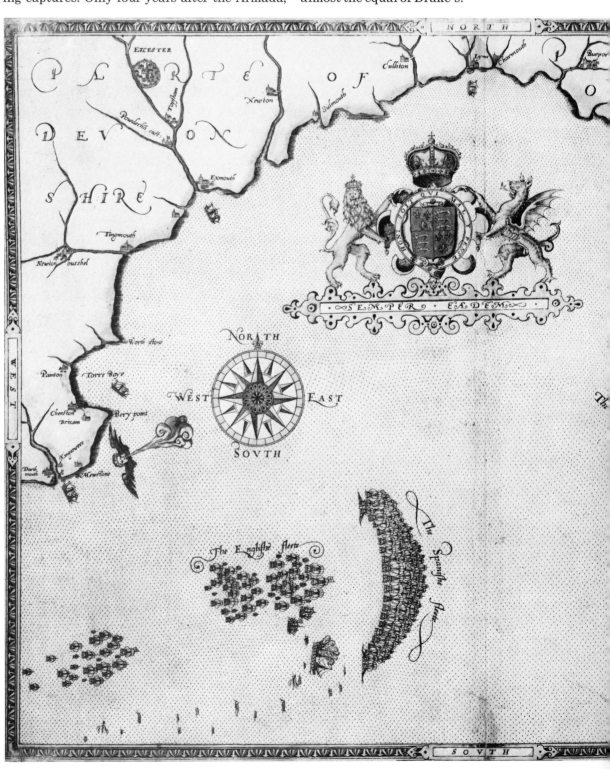

As a desperate resort Philip helped to foment trouble in Catholic Ireland, the leader being the Earl of Tyrone. Essex and Howard took Cadiz in 1596 and delayed a second Armada which was intended to bring troops and arms to help the Irish. When eventually it sailed, it was dispersed by fierce winds, as the first had been. By the time Elizabeth died, early in 1603, Philip had already been gathered to his fathers; Tyrone was on the point of submission; and it seemed as if English affairs were prospering.

The pacific policy of James I, Elizabeth's successor, was unpopular with many of his subjects, who had grown accustomed to profiting at the expense of Spain. What was worse, he neglected his navy to such an extent that sea rovers raided south coast towns and harried coastal shipping. Despite this humiliation expansion continued. Although Raleigh was unable to exploit what he described in a masterly work as 'the Large, Rich and Beautiful Empire of Guiana', others had more good fortune.

Typical of the blend of adventurer and sea officer was Sir George Somers. In Elizabeth's time he had buccaneered under Sir Amyas de Preston in the Spanish Main. In 1609, when commanding a fleet conveying settlers to Virginia, he was shipwrecked, together with Sir Thomas Gates, on the Bermudas. Somers annexed this cluster of uninhabited islands in the name of King James, and after his death they were administered for some years by Gates. The

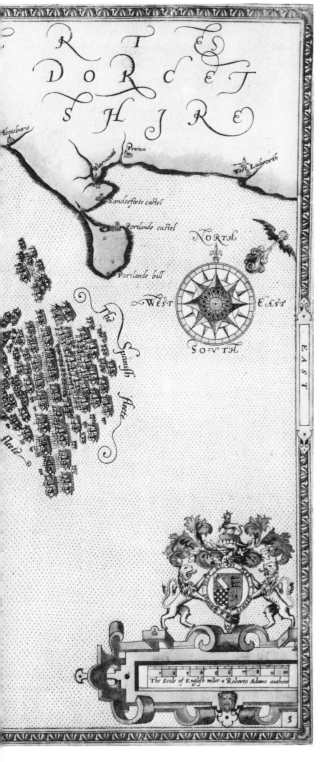

The Ld. Admirall Howard Knighting Thomas Howard, the Lord Sheffeild, Rog: Townseni Iohn Hawkins, and Martin Forbisher for their good service

An English playing-card showing Lord Howard knighting sea commanders during the Armada fight. *National Maritime Museum, Greenwich.*

first, unintentional settlers found the climate congenial, and had the good luck to light upon an enormous and very valuable lump of ambergris which started them on the way to prosperity.

The Bermuda episode was commemorated by Silvester Jourdain, who had been one of the Somers party, and his account became known to Shakespeare. Always alive to the topical allusion, the dramatist used it to help with the background of his final play, *The Tempest,* which appeared a year after the actual event. Shakespeare's isle

. . . full of noises,
Sounds and sweet airs, that give delight and
*   hurt not . . .*

would have appealed to those with a turn of mind for discovery. Certainly it was not long before Englishmen began to settle in the West Indies, the first of them at St Kitts, then others at Barbados and elsewhere. In Barbados there was a deliberate and permanent encroachment on Spanish preserves, and by the time it had gained momentum, the Dutch and the French were also very much rivals for island rights. 'I would like to see the clause in Adam's will', François I is said to have exclaimed, 'which excludes me from my share of the world.'

It was in every way sad that James I's eldest

son, Prince Frederick Henry, died of typhoid at the age of eighteen. He had been an admirer of Raleigh, who had composed his history of the world partly for the Prince's instruction, and he would have imbued him with a strong idea of the importance of sea affairs. Charles, the new heir, was aware of England's dependence on maritime traffic, and the fruitless journey he made to Spain to seek the hand of Princess Maria doubtless confirmed it.

Charles commissioned from Phineas and Peter Pett, leading shipwrights of their time, the most magnificent vessel yet built in England, the *Sovereign of the Seas*. One of his justifications was the fact that the Armada flagship, which had been renamed *Anne Royal* in 1608 in honour of his mother, Anne of Denmark, had been wrecked in 1636 after nearly half a century afloat. She was a good instance of the longevity of wooden ships, if the materials were well chosen, and the vessel properly cared for.

The Lord Admiral, Howard, was himself almost as remarkable a survival, for he lived until 1624 when he was nearly ninety. Elizabeth had made him an earl on his return from Cadiz in 1596 and she envied, though she never received, the tapestries of the Armada which Howard commissioned from the Dutch artist Hendrick Cornelisz Vroom. Howard, whose office had become quasi-hereditary, was bought out by a royal favourite,

A sixteenth-century draft
of a ship, with her sail
plan, from the collection
of Samuel Pepys.
Pepysian Library,
Magdalene College,
Cambridge.

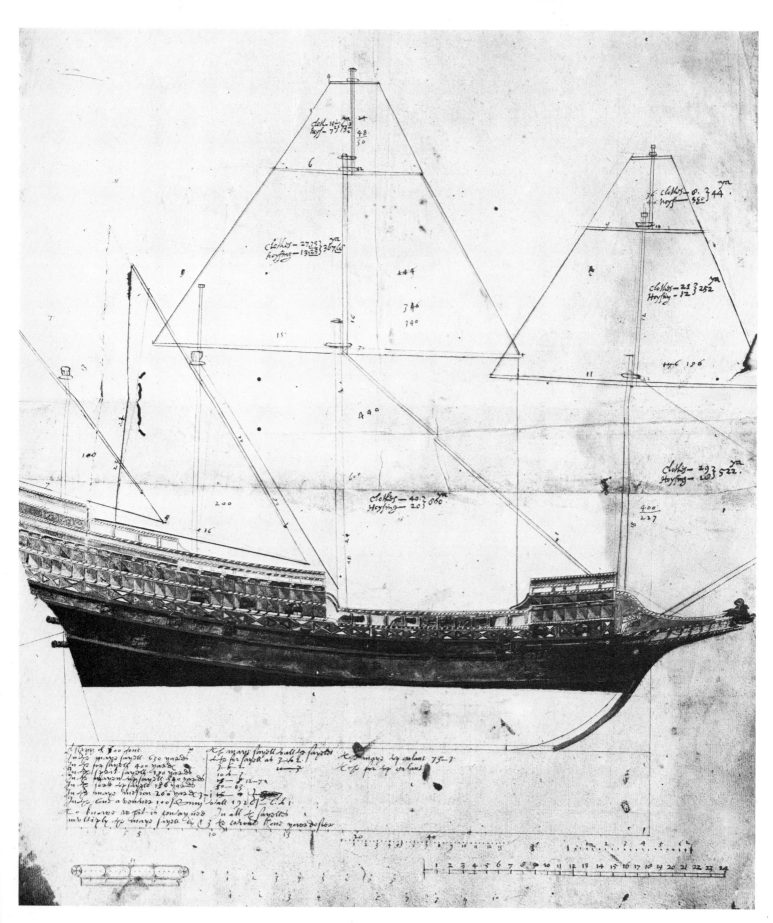

Buckingham, in 1619, but while he was alive he was a reminder of past glory.

Charles's insistence that inland as well as coastal counties should contribute to the cost of his fleet led to trouble over Ship Money. This became one of the many points of dispute between King and Parliament, which eventually led to the Civil War spanning the sad years between 1642, when Charles raised his standard at Nottingham, and 1648 when he was executed. One of the many reasons for the King's lack of success was the fact that the bulk of the navy adhered to Parliament, which was in a better position to pay the sailors. Parliament found an able strategist and manager in Robert Rich, Earl of Warwick. Charles could not match him, either in skill or resources.

This was a serious setback for the Royalist cause, since Charles depended, as Parliament did not, on regular communication with sympathisers abroad. The Queen went overseas and Charles relied on her to raise help and supplies from friendly courts. Moreover, if the King were to draw forces from Ireland, where he had a strong party, these could not be embarked if Parliament commanded the sea passages.

For its part, Parliament took over a respectable naval force, for Charles had built some good ships during his period of absolute rule. Warwick made admirable use of them, though even he could not always pay the men regularly and at one stage had desertion to cope with. In the end the task was mastered, and one by one the remaining Royalist squadrons were eliminated. The most elusive and well handled was that under Prince Rupert, cavalry commander turned admiral, and always a man to be reckoned with, as may be seen in his use of the concealed time-bomb, a stratagem far in advance of its age.

Rupert was at Lisbon in 1650, where he was watched by Blake, with a Parliamentarian fleet. On 13 April he sent a Portuguese boat to sell oil and fruit to the *Leopard,* a Parliament ship. It was manned by two negroes, and an Englishman disguised as a Portuguese. A cask of oil was duly sold, but in hoisting it aboard, the Englishman swore in his own tongue, and was thereupon seized. The cask was found to contain, 'a bomb-ball in a double headed barrel, with a lock in the bowels to give fire to a quick-match'; or it could be activated by a spring 'to be pulled by the boatman, so that it would take fire and blow up the ship.' The seaman had been promised £100 to plant this ingenious weapon.

Among the more important legislation passed under the Commonwealth was the Navigation Act of 1651. Its aim was to encourage English shipping, since it ordained that goods should be brought to the country only in English vessels or in those of the country in which they were produced. This was a blow at the carrying trade of the Dutch, which was immense, world wide and growing. The English and the Dutch, as Protestants, had fought side by side more than once

Robert Blake, 'General-at-Sea' under the Commonwealth and one of the greatest leaders England produced. A portrait of 1645. *National Maritime Museum, Greenwich.*

against the Spaniards. It was tragic that two such vigorous nations, who cherished independence and saw their future prosperity depended upon trade, should have become antagonists. But the differences went deep and they lasted until the accession of William of Orange.

War was actually declared in 1652 and during the course of it both sides discovered good leaders. The Dutch produced the elder Tromp; the English called upon Monck, once a Royalist, Penn, Deane and, above all, Robert Blake. All the Englishmen had been trained as soldiers, and they were officially described as 'Generals-at-Sea'. There was fighting in the Channel, in the North Sea and in the Mediterranean. Fortunes varied, as could have been expected with such stout ships and men. The conflict lasted two years, and led to the death of Deane in 1653 off Sole Bay, and of Tromp off Scheveningen the same year. Evertsen kept the Dutchman's flag flying so that his men should not lose heart.

The struggle was scarcely over when Cromwell, who had become Lord Protector, declared war on Spain. It was ill managed, except by Blake, who blockaded Cadiz in the Elizabethan tradition and then destroyed a Spanish squadron at Santa Cruz, Tenerife. It was his last action, for he died on his way home. His stature is undisputed, and Clarendon, a political opponent but a fair-minded one, wrote his epitaph. Blake was the first, he said, 'that infused that proportion of courage into the seamen, by making them see by experience what mighty things they could do, if they were resolved'.

Penn and an incompetent general, Robert Venables, were sent to attack the Spanish West Indian island of San Domingo, then known as Hispaniola. They failed ignominiously, but blundered into capturing Jamaica, which was retained. At first it was valued little. Later it became one of the most important bases for the British fleet. Cromwell, hearing accounts of the

right
George Monck, later Duke of Albemarle (1608–1670), land and sea commander under the Commonwealth and Charles II, by Sir Peter Lely.
National Maritime Museum, Greenwich (Greenwich Hospital Collection).

far right
Prince Rupert (1619–1682), land and sea commander, by Sir Peter Lely.
National Maritime Museum, Greenwich (Greenwich Hospital Collection).

below
A model of the *Prince* of 1670, one of the finest extant. The *Prince* was broken up in 1692, when her sounder timbers were used to build the *Royal William*, which was afloat until 1813.
Science Museum, London.

opposite, top left
Elizabeth I, a portrait by the leading miniaturist, Nicholas Hilliard.
National Portrait Gallery, London.

opposite, top right
Sir Francis Drake (*c.* 1540–1596), admiral and circumnavigator, by Nicholas Hilliard.
National Portrait Gallery, London.

opposite, bottom
The *Great Harry*, a ship of 1546, as shown in the Anthony Rolls, part of the collection of Samuel Pepys.
Pepysian Library, Magdalene College, Cambridge.

44

The Armada fight, as imagined by a contemporary artist. On the extreme right is Lord Howard of Effingham's *Ark Royal*; in the centre, with yellow and red stripes, the *Rainbow*, commanded by Lord Henry Seymour; to the right of centre, with broken mast, the *Nuestra Senora del Rosario*, the first ship to be captured by the British. Queen Elizabeth is depicted in the town (Plymouth) in the corner.
Worshipful Society of Apothecaries, London.

above
Fire-ship attack on the
Spanish Fleet, 28 July
1588.
*National Maritime
Museum, Greenwich.*

right
Peter Pett, with the
Sovereign of the Seas
(1637), the masterpiece of
the Caroline shipwrights.
*National Maritime
Museum, Greenwich.*

A model by Robert Spence
of the *Naseby*, 80 guns,
built in 1655, renamed
Royal Charles in 1660, and
captured by the Dutch in
1667.
*Lent to the Science
Museum, London, by
Robert Spence Esq.*

below
The *Royal Charles*
brought to Holland after
capture in 1667, by
Ludolf Backhuysen.
*National Maritime
Museum, Greenwich.*

opposite, top
A view of Plymouth in
1676 by the Bohemian
artist Wenceslaus Hollar.
*National Maritime
Museum, Greenwich.*

opposite, bottom
Sir George Rooke
(1650–1709) by Michael
Dahl. By his capture of
Gibraltar in 1704, Rooke
gained a Mediterranean
base of priceless value.
*National Maritime
Museum, Greenwich
(Greenwich Hospital
Collection).*

expedition, felt so angry that when Penn and Venables returned they were sent to the Tower. But when Cromwell realised their difficulties, and the toll that sickness had taken, he came to the conclusion that they had done their best, and let them go.

It was a very long time after men-of-war had been satisfactorily equipped with heavy guns, thanks to the ability of shipwrights such as James Baker, that sea commanders learned how best to use what they had at their disposal. The broadside made the old tactic of line abreast obsolete. Deane, an artillerist, taught his gunners to fire faster and more accurately than the Dutch; and the fuller answer, slowly and painfully evolved, was that of fighting in line ahead – that is, to engage on a line of bearing parallel to that of the enemy. Blake and Monck understood this, and it was the method which eventually beat Tromp. But it was never easy to establish any new doctrine among conservative and sometimes stupid captains, who had been brought up in the older way of engagement by groups, led by a divisional admiral.

Signalling at sea was still in its infancy, and would remain in a state of arrested development until the latter half of the eighteenth century. The tyranny of the permanent Fighting Instruction, with its attendant advantages and drawbacks, had yet to come. Tactical doctrine, exalted into a creed, would in time exert an inhibiting effect on all but the most independent commanders. Under such experienced men as Blake and Monck the *mêlée* was sought at sea, and it was often achieved. Then training and steady courage came into their own.

When Charles II returned to England, and to the throne, he was in the happy position of being able to take over a fine fleet. His interest in everything which concerned the sea was never in doubt. From his boyhood he had loved sailing, and his attention to naval affairs was equalled only by that of his brother James, and his cousin Prince Rupert.

Charles engaged in two campaigns against the Dutch. The first led to the capture of some of his best ships, which had misguidedly been laid up, and to the humiliation of seeing de Ruyter, with

his fleet, in control of the approaches to London. The second, in alliance with France, was highly unpopular and largely futile.

The neglected Queen, Catherine of Braganza, had brought Charles Bombay in 1662 as part of her dowry, for Portugal was regaining independence with the help of France. Bombay, with one of the finest harbours of the East, was to prove a great asset to the East India Company, which had been given its first Charter under Elizabeth. The Company already had 'factories' or depots at Surat, and at Madras on the Coromandel Coast.

The bigotry and stubbornness of James II lost him his kingdom; the Revolution of 1688 expelled him and his Catholic heirs and brought a Dutch prince to the English throne. Under the strategic guidance of William of Orange, England and Holland took part in a protracted struggle to check the power of Louis XIV, which had become as threatening as that of Spain during the previous century.

Anglo-Dutch friendship continued throughout the reign of Queen Anne, which was as glorious, in a military sense, as that of Elizabeth I. On land there were Marlborough's victories. At sea it was notable for the capture of Gibraltar in 1704 by a combined fleet, in which the principal commander was Sir George Rooke. French and Spanish were at that time allied, but French intervention helped little at sea. Once secured, Gibraltar was firmly held, and it has not been relinquished. According to the diary of Sir John Leake, of the *Prince George*: 'at 4 o'clock on 23 July the Prince of Hesse summoned the town from the north gate, where the Marines were encamped, and soon after the Admiral did the same from the south gate where the seamen were, and received the answer from the Governor that he would capitulate.' No efforts, however furious, could dislodge the combined force.

It was just over a century since the Dutch admiral Heemskirk had fought the Spaniards, also at Gibraltar, and annihilated them, though he lost his own life in the battle. This second victory was of the utmost significance, for it gave Britain the key to the western Mediterranean. It would have pleased the Elizabethan commanders that the triumph was shared with the Dutch, without whose help the defeat of the Armada would not have been nearly so complete.

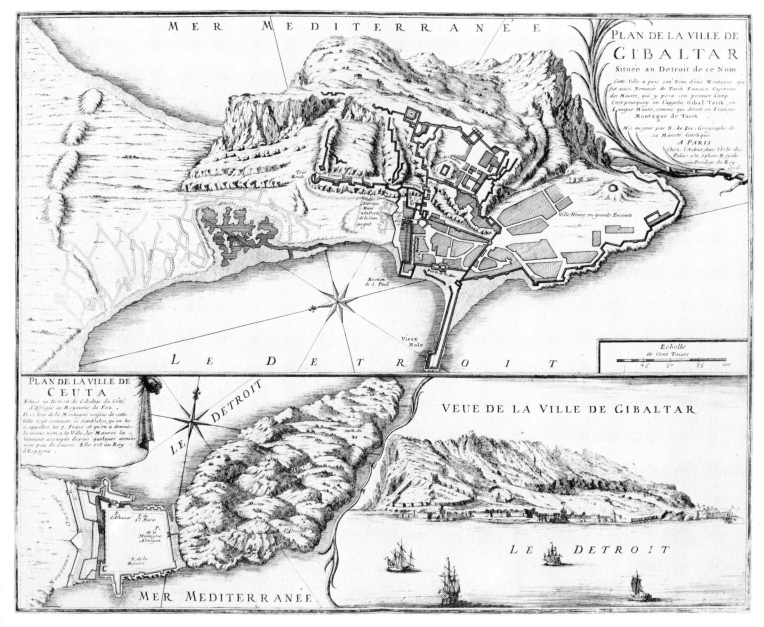

THE
DUTCH FLEET

Among those in Europe who did not rejoice at the Christian success at Lepanto were what became known as the 'Sea Beggars', the amphibious, hardy and fiercely independent-minded Protestants who inhabited what was to become known as the Dutch Republic. Only a few months after the battle, the Sea Beggars attacked the Spaniards at Brill, and it is from this incident that the beginning of their success is dated. Four years earlier, the Duke of Alva had crushed a rising with ruthless severity and had instituted a reign of terror. This the Dutch defied. Although they later learnt toleration, which their overlords never could, they had a saying *Liever Turcx dan Paaps* – 'better Turkish than Popish', which would have profoundly shocked Philip II had he ever heard it.

Dutch advantage at Brill was followed up by a defeat of the Spanish admiral Bossu off Hoorn in the Zuider Zee in 1573, at which the Dutch navy may be said to have come into being. Then and later the fleets raised in the country would have local affiliations, and be subject to local directives, which made central control a matter of some difficulty.

In considering the establishment of the fleet of Holland, one fact stands out as being of the utmost significance. Unlike any of the other countries which have raised and equipped fleets formidable enough to have made an impact upon the world, Holland had no forests to supply the shipwrights with material. Yet Dutch prosperity has always depended on ships and water. It was through the sea that she won her independence. It is by water, to a degree which is not matched elsewhere, that she lives and flourishes. The fireside idea of windmill, dyke, bridge, barge and farm remains valid to the extent that it is to engineering, conservation of resources, agriculture, shipbuilding, suitably geared to current technical advances, that the Dutch must look if they are to keep their proper place in the scheme of things. That knowledge is inborn in everyone native to Holland, and it has always been so.

The Dutch depended heavily on Norway, which was then part of the kingdom of Denmark, and on the countries of the Baltic, for timber and naval stores; half the tonnage which paid Sound dues to the King of Denmark at Elsinore was Dutch. Elsinore (in Danish, Helsingor) was the key to the Baltic in the same way that Gibraltar was the key to the Mediterranean, but for intervals between 1563 and 1570 the passage guarded by the great castle of Kronborg was closed to traffic owing to wars between Denmark and Sweden. There was an alternative route, the Belt, but it was beset with navigational hazards, and was avoided if possible. The payment of Sound dues, although an imposition, was thought to be justified by captains who regularly used the Baltic.

If the Sound was temporarily closed, there was always the ocean at large. The Dutch were early in reaching far places. This was remarkable when one considers the small population, which was perhaps one third that of England, the province of Holland itself, with 670,000, having about twice that of London, and their dependence on imports in so many vital fields. By 1599 Olivier van der Doort had sailed round the world. Three years later a Dutch East India Company was established. Within little more than a decade it was operating over fifty ships, as against England's twelve, although the English East India Charter was earlier. It had been granted largely because the Dutch, who had cornered the market in the commodity, raised the price of pepper unacceptably.

By the time they had a navy, the Dutch were developing a source of wealth, long exploited by the Venetians, which was still more profitable, because far better managed, than the flow of precious metals which the Spaniards extracted from the mines of South America. This was spices. They learnt from the Portuguese of the small bulk of spice cargoes and their enormous value. In days when people had to do without tea, coffee, chocolate, tobacco, quinine, vanilla, and when even sugar was rare, they longed for alleviation from the salt diet imposed of necessity during the winter months.

Food could be rendered more palatable and varied by the pepper and ginger of Malabar; by cardamon from the damp district of Tellicherry; by cinnamon from Ceylon. Beyond the Bay of Bengal there was opium, the only effective pain-

killer then known. There was frankincense and indigo; camphor in Borneo; nutmeg and mace in Amboyna; and in two small islands Ternate and Tidor, there grew the clove tree, surpassing most other products in value. All these commodities were so cheap on the spot and so dear in the markets of the north, as to constitute the most desirable trade in the world. The Dutch discovered, again from the Portuguese, that a voyage lasting two years, out and home, might cost, with the ship, about £4,000. But the freight might yield as much as £150,000. It was this knowledge which compelled the Dutch to provide armed escorts for their carrying trade. This was a reason, the best of all, for a strong navy, besides being the source through which it was maintained.

Philip's answer was to close the ports of Spain and Portugal to Dutch ships, which made the rebels more determined than ever to strengthen their links with the Mediterranean. They had an agent active at Leghorn by the end of the sixteenth century, one of whose concerns was the export of Tuscan marble. Thus it came about that when Louis XIV wanted marble for his place at Versailles, he bought the stone in Amsterdam. The Mediterranean interest was of course the reason for Heemskirk's fight at Gibraltar in 1607. He was defending his country's trade.

Heemskirk's was a defensive victory, helpful

to Dutchmen using the southern routes, including those undertaking the long voyage to the Far East via the Cape of Good Hope. An even shrewder blow was dealt the Spaniards in 1628, seven years after the foundation of a Dutch West India Company. Piet Hein realised the dream of every Dutch adventurer when he captured the Spanish silver fleet at Matanzas, off the north coast of Cuba, where it was assembling for the crossing to Europe. The feat made him not only rich, but one of the permanent heroes of Dutch folklore. Fifteen million florins were brought back to Holland, one of the great windfalls of naval history.

This was not the end of Spanish humiliation, for in 1639 there occurred the battle of the Downs, the first occasion on which Marten Harpertzoon Tromp became known to Europe at large. Tromp was the son of one of Heemskirk's frigate captains and was only eight years old when he first served at sea. He spent two and a half years in slavery in North Africa after being captured by an English-born pirate. Once released he soon made his name feared wherever he sailed in time of war.

One of Tromp's most brilliant exploits was to surprise a Spanish naval squadron near Gravelines, and to destroy it with the finality of Heemskirk at Gilbraltar. He then proceeded to blockade Dunkirk, whence the Spaniards had come. In order to relieve the port, the Spaniards assembled a fleet of seventy-seven ships, many of them Portuguese, with Admiral d'Oquendo in command. He was the son of the officer who had served with the Armada, and his further task was to convey 24,000 soldiers in fifty transports, nine of which had been hired from England, as reinforcements for an army engaged in the Low Countries.

The Spaniards assumed that d'Oquendo, in spite of hostility on the part of the French, would have a clear run up the Channel and that, with his greatly superior force, he would be able to brush Tromp aside. The Dutchman, who at that time held the proud title of Lieutenant-Admiral of Holland, thought otherwise. He had light forces continually on the watch between Dunkirk and the western entrance to the Channel, and on 16 September, just over half a century after the ships of Philip II had been reported off the coast of Cornwall, d'Oquendo came into view. He was off Selsey Bill, and he was keeping his ships in that disciplined order and compactness which had been a feature of the tactics of Medina Sidonia.

When the first clash occurred, Tromp had only seventeen ships in company with him, as the greater part of his fleet was still off Dunkirk. But the Dutchman, believing in taking and keeping the initiative, went into the attack. D'Oquendo,

opposite page
The obverse of a medal with a portrait of Piet Hein, commemorating his capture of the Spanish treasure fleet in 1628. *National Maritime Museum, Greenwich.*

below
A commemorative painting of 1622 by Cornelis van Wieringen of a battle near Gibraltar fought in 1607 between Dutch and Spaniards. *National Maritime Museum, Greenwich.*

with superior numbers and a favouring wind, at first stood up boldly, and at one time had Tromp almost surrounded. The Dutch then made a set at the Spanish flagship, the *Santiago,* which received some damage. D'Oquendo, who had given no instructions to his captains as to how they should proceed, allowed himself, when the wind changed, to retreat across Channel. He took refuge off Dover, realising that he could no longer hope to relieve Dunkirk without a major battle.

D'Oquendo anchored close to an English squadron commanded by Sir John Pennington. This Englishman had served a sea apprenticeship under Sir Robert Mansell, who had fought alongside Tromp's predecessors against Philip. He promptly got the Spaniards taken out of the English hired transports, precipitating an extremely tense situation. For here were two hostile fleets, the larger of them at anchor in the waters of a neutral country, whose admiral refused to allow either Spanish or Dutch admirals to fly their flags.

English sympathies were divided. People and seamen were mainly for the Dutch, but the Court inclined towards the Spaniards, and d'Oquendo was permitted to send ashore for water and supplies, for which he was charged exorbitantly. Tromp was soon reinforced, though his numbers did not at first exceed thirty. Weeks passed, and then, singly and in pairs, some of the bolder Spanish captains, under cover of night, stole away to ports in Flanders.

At last Tromp, with an insolence which should have roused d'Oquendo's pride and fury, offered to send the Spaniards 500 barrels of gunpowder to fight it out with him. He had already despatched a series of urgent messages to the five Dutch Admiralties–Rotterdam, Amsterdam, North Quarter, Middleburg and Friesland–asking them to strain every nerve to send him as many ships as possible.

An engraving of Piet Hein's capture of the Spanish treasure fleet off Havana in 1628. *National Maritime Museum, Greenwich.*

The response was immediate. Work went forward ceaselessly in the dockyards and within less than a month Tromp had over a hundred sail at his command, including fireships. Most of them were smaller than those of the Spaniards, but size in itself was nothing. He became so confident about the result of an attack that he told an Englishman that King Charles would soon have all the Spaniards' guns, his countrymen their ships, and the Devil their men. Boasts by admirals and generals are rash, but in this case Tromp was justified.

His patience at last exhausted, and his strength more than adequate, Tromp detached Admiral Witte de With to watch Pennington, in case the English should try to interfere. Then, on 21 October, he himself bore down on the Spaniards with the cream of his fleet, the Dutch tricolour flying proudly from the main masthead of the flagship.

There has seldom been a victory more complete. D'Oquendo and the best of his captains fought stubbornly, but as the Spaniard had still contrived no tactical plan, either for attack or defence, his ships went one by one like sheep to the slaughter. Almost the whole Spanish force was burnt, run ashore or captured. At least 7,000 men are known to have perished, many of them in the galleon *San Theresa*, which was one of the victims of fire. The Dutch losses were trifling.

Tromp in the *Amelia* engaged d'Oquendo in the *Santiago*. The Spaniard managed to get away under cover of mist but it was the most he could do. He made for Dunkirk, from before which port the Dutch had by then withdrawn. Only thirteen ships managed to join their leader, and when they came to assess the damage which they had suffered, they found that the *Santiago* alone had 1,700 shot holes. Other ships had come off nearly as badly. Before the winter set in d'Oquendo returned to Spain, as dejected as his father had been after the Armada.

The battle not only ensured the lasting fame of

A medal by J Looff commemorating the battle of the Downs, 1639. *National Maritime Museum, Greenwich.*

Marten Tromp; it made Holland dominant in northern waters, and it was one of the factors which forced Spain to recognise Dutch independence, which was agreed in 1648 at the Peace of Münster. It was some years before her position was challenged, and with England engaged in civil war Holland had the opportunity to extend her influence. Yet her position of dependence on other countries for so large a proportion of her own needs created difficulties and involved her in further conflicts. The first of them was with England.

The struggle arose not only out of the difficulties caused by the Navigation Act passed by the English Commonwealth Parliament with the aim of curbing what was virtually a Dutch monopoly in the carrying trade, but because of English insistence on the right to search neutral ships for contraband in time of war. Insistence on saluting the English flag was also made a point of substance, which was irritating to proud men. There was also the possibility that, taking advantage of the difficulties of the King of Denmark, who faced an aggressive Sweden, the Dutch might try to farm the Sound dues at Elsinore, to the disadvantage of shipping not their own.

Although the Dutch were in the end defeated in their war with England, the earlier encounters went mainly in their favour, and what finally decided the issue as much as any other single factor was the different attitudes shown by the two governments towards the respective sea commanders. At one stage, Dutch directives and post-mortems on operations so infuriated and handicapped Tromp that he was moved to write in exasperation: 'my trouble arises from this, that after I have given all that is in me to the service of my country, I may be molested on my return home with subtle questions'. How many admirals, before and since Tromp's time, have echoed his complaint, and with what justice! Very different was the attitude of Oliver Cromwell, who had strategic charge of operations and who had himself experienced the perplexities which may beset a commander-in-chief. He trusted his admirals, Blake particularly, to such a degree that he wrote: 'you must handle the reins as you shall find your opportunity, and the ability of the Fleet, to be'. Such was the confidence between two supremely competent men, who knew that what really mattered in both sea and land campaigning, was how things appeared to the tactical commander on the spot.

Tromp's other complaint, which again is echoed down the centuries, was of laggard captains, who either did not understand his instructions, or who were 'shy' in supporting their fellow officers when attacked by the enemy. He was also sometimes short of men. This was scarcely to be wondered at, for while the volume of Dutch shipping, men-of-war and merchantmen, was such that they had more ships afloat than Spain, Portugal, France and England combined, manpower to work them was a constant

60

right
Admiral Cornelisz de With (1599–1658), distinguished in the fighting with Sweden, in which he was killed. *Nederlandsch Historisch Scheepvaartmuseum, Amsterdam.*

below
The battle of the Sound, 1658, with inset portraits of Admirals Wassenaer of Holland (left) and Wrangel of Sweden (right). *National Maritime Museum, Greenwich.*

difficulty. At least 80,000 sailors were needed, or 10% of the male population of the Dutch provinces. Recruitment was made up by volunteers from the Scandinavian countries and from northern Germany. There was also what was known as the Great Fishery, upon which so much of Dutch prosperity depended, and which was greatly interfered with by the war.

The movement of the shoals of herring from the Baltic to the North Sea in the later Middle Ages, and the discovery of improved means of salting and curing them, had stimulated the Dutch into a regular cycle of activity which had become of the utmost importance. Fishermen sailed from Holland in their *buizen* or 'busses', as contemporary Englishmen called them, and, starting in the Shetlands on St John's day, 24 June, they fished their way southwards, often within sight of the Scottish and English coasts, until they reached the mouth of the Thames about the beginning of December. Their boats were specialised in construction, being large and decked. They carried salt on board, and were thus able to wait for bigger catches than inshore fishermen, while the ships remained economical to operate. One of the results of Philip's closure of the ports of Spain to the Dutch was that these adventurous people ventured across the Atlantic to seek extra salt for the Great Fishery on the

PRÆLIUM NAVALE INTER BELGAS ET SUECOS. Aº 1658.

shores of Venezuela. This was part of that process of infiltration which led to Dutch settlements in Guiana, Curaçao, Brazil and elsewhere within territory formally forbidden them. They were intruders who became ever more difficult to dislodge.

By far the best-known type of Dutch ship was the *fluyt*, which was round-sterned, flat-bottomed and relatively narrow. The Sound dues were then based on a tonnage system which was calculated partly on the bulk of a vessel amidships. For this reason the *fluyts,* which played their part in war as supply ships and auxiliaries, were built with their sides sloping sharply inwards. When a new scheme of measurement was introduced in 1669, the decks gradually became broader.

With regard to ships of war built as such, while the English and French laid down many three-decked vessels during the seventeenth and later centuries, the Dutch did so far less often. For one thing, such monsters used up an inordinate amount of timber, so precious in Holland, and for another, they were difficult to handle in the shallow waters off the Dutch coast. Dutch ships in general were lighter than those of the English, but although this made them swifter and more manoeuvrable, it could be disastrous when they came under heavy gunfire.

Even so, Dutch construction became the model for most other powers. Peter the Great, when he set about his task of studying the main principles of western technology, gave himself wholeheartedly to copying the shipwrights of Zaandam, while French, Swedes, Danes and Germans were among those who were most eager to profit

A fine contemporary model of the Dutch *Zeelandia* of 1653. *Maritime Museum 'Prins Hendrik', Rotterdam.*

from Dutch skill. In common with most other seafaring countries, the Dutch were accomplished in what the English called 'ginger-bread' work, the elaborate ornamentation of sterns, usually in the baroque style, with lions, soldiers, cupids, caryatids and heraldic achievements much in evidence. At the opening of the seventeenth century the stern was often topped by a single enormous lantern. Later there were commonly three and sometimes five. The Dutch also used wind-driven saw-mills, which helped in keeping down costs and thus making the prices of their ships attractive to foreign buyers.

They enjoyed little respite from war at sea. The conflict with England was not long finished before they were compelled to fight Sweden, in order to ensure that the Sound dues should not become a Swedish rather than a Danish monopoly. For while the Kings of Denmark, profiting as they did from the handsome income derived from Elsinore, had as a rule favoured the Dutch as their best customers, Sweden might prove a very different matter. Her sovereigns, ambitious for conquest, were determined not to allow the Baltic to become open to all comers. They had in mind a Swedish lake.

In their attitude towards the matter of the Sound, Dutch and English coincided absolutely;

so much so that, after the death of Oliver Cromwell, his feeble son Richard was quite prepared to send a fleet, if he could raise the money, to support English interests in the Baltic. By 1658 Charles X of Sweden had made it apparent that he intended to control both shores of the Sound, and not merely his own. It was then that van Bueningen, the Dutch representative at the Court of King Frederick III of Denmark, spoke out. He made the boast, concerning his country's fleet, that 'the oaken keys of the Sound lie in the docks of Amsterdam'. This was a neat way of saying that, if it came to the pinch, the Dutch would be ready to fight to maintain the *status quo* at Elsinore. Van Bueningen was soon called upon to make good his words.

The Dutch had already won one round with Charles X. In 1656 the Swedes had besieged Danzig. This was an action which affected Holland closely, for Danzig was the centre of a huge corn-carrying complex. Under pressure from the merchants of Amsterdam, Admiral Obdam was sent through the Sound with a fleet of forty-two well-equipped ships, and in due course he raised the siege. Thus checked, Charles X renewed relations with Holland, albeit uneasily, and Danzig was declared a neutral port.

Charles then struck at Denmark. He invaded

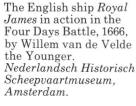

The English ship *Royal James* in action in the Four Days Battle, 1666, by Willem van de Velde the Younger. *Nederlandsch Historisch Scheepvaartmuseum, Amsterdam.*

left
Marten Harpertzoon
Tromp (1597–1653), one of
the great sea commanders
of Dutch history.
*Nederlandsch Historisch
Scheepvaartmuseum,
Amsterdam.*

below
The Spanish flagship is
destroyed at the battle of
Gibraltar, 1607. By
Hendrik Cornelisz Vroom.
*Rijksmuseum,
Amsterdam.*

The Dutch attack British ships in the Medway in
1667, by P C van Soest.
National Maritime Museum, Greenwich.

the country, drove Frederick's fleet from the sea, placed a garrison at Elsinore, and prepared to besiege Copenhagen. It was high time for the second round.

It began in October 1658 when Obdam, with thirty-five ships carrying 4,000 troops, was ordered north with the object of destroying the Swedish fleet and relieving the Danish capital. The clash of arms occurred on 29 October at the entrance to the Sound. Wrangel, the Swedish commander, was numerically the stronger and the battle, as could have been expected from the characters of the commanders and the importance of the issue to be decided, was fierce and bloody. Obdam had organised his force into three squadrons, the van under de With, the centre under his own eye, and the rear under Floriszoon. There was a Danish squadron ready to support the Dutch, but head winds did not allow it to leave Copenhagen at the crucial time.

The action developed into a series of ship-to-ship encounters at very close quarters. De With, in the *Brederode*, made straight for Wrangel, who flew his flag in the much larger *Victoria*. But when Obdam came up in the *Eendracht*, de With engaged two ships nearer his own weight of metal. One was the *Drake*, the other the *Leopard*. The *Leopard* was so badly damaged that she ran

ashore and was burnt. Both the *Drake* and the *Brederode* grounded on the Danish shore. The *Drake* got off, but the *Brederode* at first remained fast. She was attacked by the *Wismar* and was boarded after a bombardment lasting two hours. De With was killed and his ship captured, but shortly afterwards she slipped into deeper water and foundered.

Wrangel's flagship meanwhile had suffered so greatly from Obdam's attack that the Swede had to take her out of action to Helsingør, where she anchored for repairs. Obdam was later in danger from four Swedish ships which made a concerted assault, and he was rescued only after some difficulty. In the close fighting round or near the *Eendracht*, Admiral Floriszoon was killed.

The battle had begun at about nine o'clock in the morning. By the early afternoon the wind had freshened, and the Dutch fleet ran down to Copenhagen. Although Obdam had not annihilated his opponent, he was able to relieve the Danish city. The Swedes lost five ships: three captured, one captured and sunk, one run ashore and burnt. On the other hand, the Dutch had lost two of their best admirals.

The war did not end until the following year, when Michel de Ruyter, who shares with the elder Tromp the leading place in Dutch naval

One of the clashes
between Dutch and
English in the Four Days
Battle of 1666. Dutch
flagship (centre); British
flagship (right). By
Abraham Storck.
*National Maritime
Museum, Greenwich.*

history, sailed with a large fleet and 12,000 troops to follow up the advantage gained by Obdam. The idea of a northern hegemony dominated by Sweden was doomed. Charles X died early in 1660, and although the peace treaty was on the whole favourable to Sweden, the Dutch secured their right of passage through the Sound on what they knew as their 'Mother Trade' with the Baltic, while Elsinore was restored to Danish possession. The Dutch, led by Cornelius Tromp, the famous admiral's son, and the Danes led by Niels Juel, were once more allied later in the century, but the general balance of power in the north was not affected.

The hero of the second war with the English, which arose, mainly over trade, in 1665, was undoubtedly de Ruyter. The conflict extended over two years and it included, in what was known as the Four Days Battle (1–4 June 1666), one of the most involved actions of the era. The English had divided their fleet, sending Prince Rupert, one of the joint admirals, to meet a threat from the French. Monck, left to face a much superior adversary, attacked, and although he was re-pulsed and suffered heavy losses (including two flag officers, Berkeley and Myngs, killed, and another, Ayscue, taken prisoner) he kept his forces together until Rupert could join him, after which the pair made an orderly and fighting retreat.

Humiliation, as severe as anything in naval history since the defeat of the Armada, came a year later. Charles II laid up his great ships, partly for lack of money to keep them in commission. The Dutch did not let such a golden chance go by. De Ruyter entered the Medway, carried off the splendid *Royal Charles* in which the King had returned from exile, inflicted a great deal of further damage, and paralysed the trade of London, whose citizens had already suffered

plague and fire. English pride was indeed humbled, and Charles was fortunate to be able to make a reasonably favourable peace. Both countries retained certain overseas possessions they had wrested from each other. England kept New York, once called New Amsterdam, and Holland kept Surinam. There was some relaxation of the Navigation Act in that Dutch ships were allowed henceforward to bring German and Flemish goods into English ports, as well as the produce of their own country.

Before the end of the reign of Charles II Holland faced a threat as serious as any she had suffered from the Spaniards. It was from Louis XIV, whose purpose was to extend French territory at Dutch expense. Charles was inveigled, partly due to his continuing need for money, into support of the French by sea, and a third Anglo-Dutch war occurred. By land, French armies advanced on Holland, and Dutchmen had to cut their dykes to try to save themselves. Faced with such dangers, there was dissension as well as unity in Holland. De Witte, the Grand Pensionary, was brutally murdered, and William of Orange became Stadholder.

Throughout his life, both before and after his elevation to the English throne, William had one obsessive aim. It was to defeat France. Henceforward, for more than a generation, Dutch and English were to fight side by side at sea in various parts of the world, often gloriously. They did so

above
A scene at the height of
the mêlée at Camperdown,
1797, where Dutch and
British fought for the last
time. By William
Adolphus Knell.
*National Maritime
Museum, Greenwich.*

right
Admiral Duncan
receiving the Dutch
admiral's sword after the
battle of Camperdown,
1797. By S Drummond.
*National Maritime
Museum, Greenwich
(Greenwich Hospital
Collection).*

with mutual respect, though not without those differences, sometimes acute, which so often accompany alliances.

Only twice in the future did the Dutch and English fleets meet in a hostile way. Late in the eighteenth century, during the course of the American War of Independence, Holland was for a time drawn into the struggle, since her commerce was once more suffering at British hands, and she was among the first to encourage the Americans. On 5 August 1781 there occurred a slogging match off the Dogger Bank in the North Sea, between Admirals Zoutman and Parker, after which both men, not very convincingly, claimed a victory. Just over sixteen years later, in 1797, when Holland had been drawn within the French orbit during the course of the Revolutionary and Napoleonic Wars, Admirals Duncan and de Winter clashed at Camperdown. Once again the fight was stubborn, but victory was decidedly with Duncan. He took de Winter prisoner and captured eleven prizes.

Holland managed to maintain her neutrality during the first of the two World Wars of the present century, but during the course of the Second World War, her possessions in the Far East fell to Japan and she had to call upon American sea power to regain them. Dutch seamen, allied with those of the western democracies, played a brave part in the struggle. The history of her fleet, at once her safeguard and her pride is indeed starred with great events, and she has produced some of the most redoubtable admirals who ever put to sea.

above
The interior of a Dutch submarine in the Second World War.

left
The Dutch aircraft carrier *Soemba*, operational during the Second World War.

THE SWEDISH FLEET

In the year 1625 Gustavus Adolphus, the warrior king of Sweden, ordered a man-of-war to be built at the royal shipyard of Stockholm. She was to be called the *Vasa,* after the founder of the dynasty to which Gustavus belonged. Her specifications were prepared by a Dutchman, Hendrik Hyberts-sson, who died when the vessel was still on the stocks.

By August 1628 the *Vasa* had been completed and was ready to join her country's fleet. On the 10th of the month she began her maiden voyage from the royal palace to the naval base, where a squadron was assembling. While still in the harbour she heeled so violently to a gust of wind that water poured in through the lower gun ports. The list worsened, and to the astonishment and consternation of those ashore and afloat who had greeted her appearance with pride and pleasure, she foundered in 100 feet of water, sails set and flags flying.

For 333 years the *Vasa* lay beneath the sea. After the first half century, during which some of her valuable guns were brought up, she was forgotten. She was rediscovered in 1956, when an extraordinary salvage operation began, during the course of which the resources of the Swedish navy were engaged. It was successful. The final raising and docking took place in April 1961, when archaeologists and other experts could start on the protracted task of restoration. In human terms, the loss due to the sinking of the ship had not been great. Fifteen skeletons were found during the operations, and it is thought that not more than a total of thirty perished in the tragedy. The *Vasa* is today one of the sights of Stockholm, a tangible reminder of the time when Sweden was a formidable power in Europe.

Gustavus Adolphus made his country strong by land and sea, for he was determined to extend his territory and influence. But although the king lived and died a soldier, and in the view of Napoleon, one of the greatest, it was through his maritime resources that he was able to land and to supply an army in Germany, and thus to intervene with such effect on the Protestant side during the course of the war which convulsed Europe between 1618 and 1648.

Gustavus Adolphus' reign (1611–1632) fell entirely within the sixty years during which Christian IV ruled over Denmark. Christian had come to the throne in the year of the Spanish Armada; he died the year that Charles I of England was executed. He was a prodigiously energetic and many-sided man, one of the handful of monarchs who have personally led fleets into battle. He could seldom claim success, and his sense of timing was poor, but his people made him the subject of folklore, and he is certainly the only king who ever lost the sight of an eye in a sea fight. The garments he wore on the occasion, in 1644, when he put to sea in order to save the Danish islands from falling into the hands of the Swedes, are as lovingly preserved at Rosenborg Castle, Copenhagen, as is Nelson's uniform coat at Greenwich.

Brave as he was, Christian could not prevent Swedish predominance in Baltic waters. This led in due course to the intervention of the Dutch. Denmark, which had ruled Norway since the Middle Ages, had for the future to rely mainly upon alliances to keep her status as a Baltic power. Her position was often precarious, but she managed to preserve it until she was caught up, early in the nineteenth century, in the rivalries of the great powers of the time. She then paid a price for her adherence to the cause of France.

The Treaty of Westphalia which ended the Thirty Years War made Sweden a continental as well as a Scandinavian power. She became established in western Pomerania, and she obtained Wismar, together with the duchies of Bremen and Verden. She thus had an opening on the North Sea, so that a fleet was more essential to her than ever. Unhappily, the gains she made were threatened by her rivals. She was faced with constant difficulties and became involved in a series of wars which bled the country white.

Swedish aspirations did not cease with the death of Charles X, who had clashed so disastrously with the Dutch when he had temporarily become master of both shores of the Sound; but the country had in fact reached the furthest limits of its expansion. Finland was in Swedish hands and so, on the south-eastern shore of the Baltic, were Ingria, Estonia and Livonia. Faced with such a neighbour, it was inevitable that

D · G ·
GVSTAVVS ADOLPHVS
REX SVEDIÆ · ANO
1631

right
A carved wooden lion's head from a gun port of the
Vasa.
Statens Sjöhistoriska Museum, Stockholm.

below
A reconstruction of the original appearance of the
Vasa, as she was when, setting sail on her maiden
voyage from Stockholm harbour to join the fleet of
Gustavus Adolphus, she heeled over to a gust of wind
and, rapidly flooding through her lower gun ports,
sank before the astonished eyes of the cheering
crowds.
Statens Sjöhistoriska Museum, Stockholm.

80

Denmark should make continuous efforts to bring her down, and much of the life of the austere Charles XI was spent in defending what his father had won. It was left to Charles XII, that character described by Samuel Johnson as possessing 'A frame of adamant, a soul of fire,' to create a military legend equalled only by Gustavus Adolphus among his own countrymen. Yet Charles XII, by reckless aggression against Poland and Russia, introduced a new and lasting element into the Baltic. This was Russian sea power, the importance of which was fully grasped by Peter the Great.

Early in his life, Charles XII gained a memorable victory over Peter at Narva, but it led him to false conclusions. He believed that Russia was so vulnerable that he had only to march east, with his seasoned troops and he would meet with slight resistance. Like Napoleon and Hitler he was mistaken, for not only could Russia, above all countries, trade space for time, but she has always possessed vast resources of manpower and natural capacity.

Charles was defeated in 1709 by Peter at Poltava, and was forced to seek refuge in Turkey. So confident had Peter become in the future of his country as a European power that he had already begun to build a capital at Petersburg, now Leningrad, as his 'window on the west'. He also established an Admiralty, still one of the principal sights of his great city, creating a strong navy, having himself gone to Holland and England to learn some of those technical secrets which were enabling the two countries to expand so rapidly.

For his part, so occupied had he been with his military campaigns, Charles XII had little time or money for his fleet, and it was now faced with three stiff tasks. It had to protect Sweden and her trade abroad; it had to contain Denmark; and it had to guard against Russia. If, in the end, such complex burdens were beyond its capacity, this was not because successive rulers and their admirals lacked resolution and skill.

The Baltic being an inland sea, with peculiar coastal conditions and no tides, it was a sphere for the oared galley and gunboat, which survived there as first-line fighting types long after they had disappeared elsewhere; they fought side by side with the sailing ship, of which the *Vasa* may have been an elaborate rather than a typical example. It was Finland which was most often in dispute between Sweden and Russia, and all along the north side of the Gulf of Finland there runs a strip of rocks and islands which prevents sailing ships of any great size from approaching the mainland except at a few projecting headlands. At the same time it provides a series of sheltered channels for oared craft from Viborg in the east to the Åland Island in the west. Without control of this coastal belt, a sailing fleet, however strong, could do little towards co-operating with an army ashore. The link was the rowed flotilla.

Both Sweden and Russia called upon the services of a succession of foreign experts to advise them on maritime affairs and at times to command ships or fleets. The Russians, with their greater resources, made good use of their opportunities and steadily gained the upper hand in

Kronborg Castle, Elsinore, the scene of the opening of *Hamlet*, and the key to the entrance of the Baltic by way of the Sound.

81

the Gulf of Finland, if not in the Baltic generally. In 1714, six years after Poltava, Charles' admirals were badly beaten at Hangöudde, with the result that Peter was able to occupy the eastern part of Finland without serious dispute from Sweden.

Charles was killed in action in Norway in 1718, and so was spared the humiliation of seeing the dismemberment of the larger part of the empire which his grandfather, and Gustavus Adolphus before him, had built up. The treaty of Nystadt, signed in 1720, gave Russia possession of Estonia, Livonia, Ingria, Karelia and a slice of Finland which included the fortress town of Viborg. By the time Peter died, five years later, he had made his country into the sort of sea power which had always been his ambition, with a considerable grip on both the Baltic and the Black Sea.

It then became the hope of Swedish statesmen to regain some of their lost territories, though the resources of the country were insufficient to accomplish this successfully. Sweden had one piece of good fortune when a Yorkshire shipwright called Chapman settled at Gothenburg. There he flourished, though it was his grandson, Fredrik Henrik af Chapman, later ennobled by the Swedish king, who left a permanent impres-

sion on the navy of his adopted country. He is remembered there today in the Chapmansporten, the house where he worked at Karlskrona.

Af Chapman, after an apprenticeship under his father at Gothenburg, went to England as a ship's carpenter. There he made notes and drawings so assiduously that he was regarded with suspicion, and was once arrested for espionage. He returned to Sweden in 1744 and took over a shipyard. Having made a success of this, he set out on his travels again, studying shipbuilding methods throughout Europe. In 1760 he was appointed chief shipbuilder to the Swedish navy at Karlskrona and Stockholm. Five years later he started work on his masterpiece, *Architectura Navalis Mercatoria*, with the help of his nephew, Lars Gobman. In 1776 he became a member of the Swedish Admiralty Board and principal naval architect and advisor to Gustavus III, the brilliant king who was the last European sovereign to lead a fleet into battle.

Sweden and Russia were at war for much of the eighteenth century, and af Chapman was not only a versatile and farseeing experimenter, but a practical seaman. He was able to enthuse Gustavus with his ideas, and about one of them, for a new type of gun-sloop, he reported: 'When

opposite page
The *Vasa* was salvaged in 1961. Here the interior is shown during treatment of the timbers with a preserving solution.

below
The lower gun deck of the *Vasa*, emptied of mud and undergoing restoration. The square holes in the foreground admitted light and air to the lower decks. The massive horizontal beam in the background is the bitt round which the anchor cable was lashed.

An incident at the battle
of the Sound, 1658,
showing (centre) the
sinking of a Swedish ship
and (right) fire on board
another. By Willem van
de Velde the Elder.
*Rijksmuseum,
Amsterdam.*

right
Peter the Great, Tsar of
Russia from 1682 to 1725,
who founded the Russian
tradition of a strong navy.
A portrait by Karl
Klingstadt.
*National Maritime
Museum, Greenwich.*

far right
Charles XII of Sweden
(reigned 1697–1718),
whose aggression against
Poland and Russia
provoked Peter the Great
to develop a rival naval
force in the Baltic. A
portrait of 1706 by J D
Swartz.
Sjöholm Castle, Sweden.

below
A carving of Charles XI
of Sweden (reigned
1660–1697) from the stern
of a ship.
*Statens Sjöhistoriska
Museum, Stockholm.*

these gun-sloops had been built I armed one of them myself, took it up to Värtan in Stockholm where the King himself came on board, and then rowed it, fired salvoes, made for land and set out gangplanks, landed with the guns and advanced, firing all the time, then retreated, still firing, until the guns were once more in position in the sloop. All came happily to an end, when his Majesty made me Lieutenant-Colonel.'

While af Chapman was working in Sweden, Russia enjoyed the advice and help of the inventive and talented Sir Samuel Bentham, who had been attracted to the country in 1780 by offers from Catherine the Great, and who stayed there until 1791. It was a period of great activity on the part of both Baltic and Black Sea fleets, chief command in the navy being held with distinction by a British naval officer, Sir Samuel Grieg, who had taken service early in Catherine's reign, and who remained in Russia for the rest of his life.

Several British officers commanded Russian ships of the line in wars against Sweden. One, Sir Sidney Smith, later to become famous for his defence of Acre against Napoleon Bonaparte, served Gustavus III and his admiral brother, Prince Carl, Duke of Södermanland.

During the reign of Catherine the Great, Poland was partitioned, in three stages, between Austria, Prussia and Russia. It was thus snuffed out, for a considerable time, as an independent country. One of the results was an extensive addition to Russia's Baltic seaboard and the emergence of Prussia as a potential maritime country of more than minor importance. In the future, neither could be challenged with impunity by Sweden or Denmark.

The fact was well illustrated by the events of the reign of Gustavus III, who had inherited the wish to regain what had been lost, particularly in eastern Finland. With that in mind he went to war, rashly in the view of many of his subjects, with the Russian Empress. The course of the struggle was chequered, one side or the other first gaining an advantage, and then losing it.

Among af Chapman's many services to Gustavus was the building of a vessel called the *Amphion,* which was in effect a command ship. Eloquent memorials still remain in Sweden to testify not only to the ingenuity of her construction, but also to the beauty of her fittings. It was from the *Amphion* that Gustavus liked best to exercise control during his sea campaigns.

During the summer of 1788 the Swedes, hoping to take advantage of the fact that Catherine was involved in war with Turkey, sailed up the Gulf of Finland in strength to attack Petersburg. They were repulsed, although the Russians suffered heavy losses. Gustavus then faced trouble at home, for many of his people were dissatisfied with his conduct of affairs. Denmark, seizing the opportunity of embarrassing her neighbour when she was engaged elsewhere, declared war. During the months which followed Gustavus became master of his own house through a well planned

below
Ball and charge of powder for a Swedish 12-pounder gun of the era of sail.
Statens Sjöhistoriska Museum, Stockholm.

bottom
Catherine the Great, Empress of Russia from 1762 to 1796, who employed British naval architects and officers in the Russian navy. A portrait by Michael Schebanoff.
Collection of Her Majesty Queen Elizabeth II.

87

coup d'état, and the Danes showed little activity beyond giving shelter to a Russian squadron, and putting the facilities of Copenhagen at Catherine's disposal.

By 1790, thanks to great exertions, the Swedes had been able to build up their strength at sea so that Prince Carl could be given charge of 42 ships-of-war, mainly sailing vessels. Gustavus in person commanded the oar-propelled squadrons, which consisted of 27 galleys and well over 230 gunboats, besides some troop transports. As the Danes withdrew from the war, the King could concentrate on his main opponent.

He set out from Karlskrona with his armada on 30 April 1790, very early in the year in view of the time during which ice usually remained on the surface of the Baltic. Two weeks later a Russian force was met with, under the orders of the Prince of Nassau-Siegen. In the fighting which followed one Swedish ship was captured and another sunk after gale damage, but Gustavus succeeded in his principal aim. This was to force his way into the harbour of Fredrikshamn, where he seized 29 Russian coasters and destroyed the arsenal. He also put some troops ashore at Viborg, which he hoped would serve as his base for operations against the Russian capital.

Prince Carl should have joined his brother at Viborg, but on 7 June he was attacked by a fleet under Admiral Kruse, which had sailed from Kronstadt. The battle was indecisive, but shortly afterwards Kruse was reinforced with 24 ships under Admiral Tchitchagov, which gave the

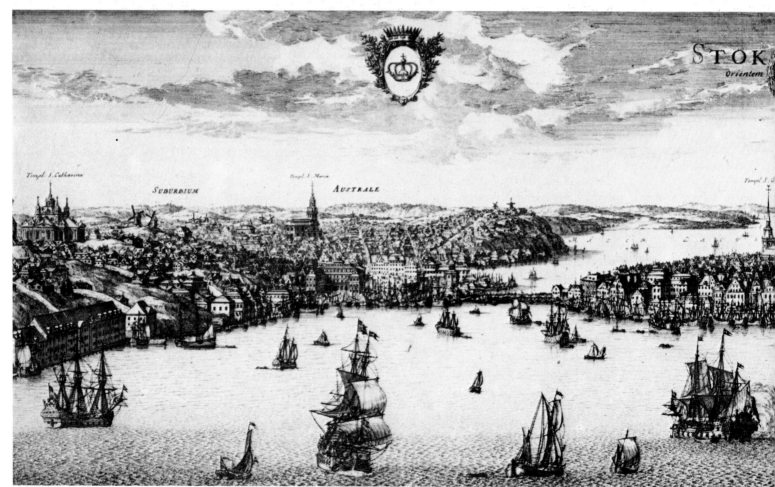

Russians overwhelming superiority. Under the circumstances, Prince Carl deemed himself fortunate to be able to reach Viborg and anchor there, although by now the Swedish troops had been withdrawn.

The Swedish fleet took up a position across the mouth of Viborg Bay. The Russians followed the same course, but anchored well out of gunshot range. Such a state of affairs could not last long, for Viborg was in fact blockaded, and as the Swedes were unable to get supplies or water from a shore which was firmly in Russian hands, it was necessary for the Prince to force his way out to sea.

On 3 July he broke out, initially inflicting more damage than he received. One of the Russian ships of the line, commanded by a British officer, James Trevenen, suffered badly, Trevenen receiving a mortal wound. Unfortunately for the Prince, when almost half his fleet had passed the Russian lines in safety, one of his fireships ran aboard a ship of the line, which in turn collided with a frigate. All three ships blew up, and the explosion added to the usual smoke resulting from a naval action, made visibility so bad that four other ships of the line, two frigates and some smaller vessels went aground and were captured. The rest escaped for the time, but two more large ships were pursued, overhauled and captured before they could reach the safety of Sveaborg, which was in Swedish hands and their principal coastal fortress.

Gustavus, with the galley fleet, also success-

The obverse of a medal of 1808 commemorating the services of F H af Chapman, a great designer of Swedish ships. By C G Fehrman. *National Maritime Museum, Greenwich.*

The reverse of the same medal showing shipwrightry by af Chapman.

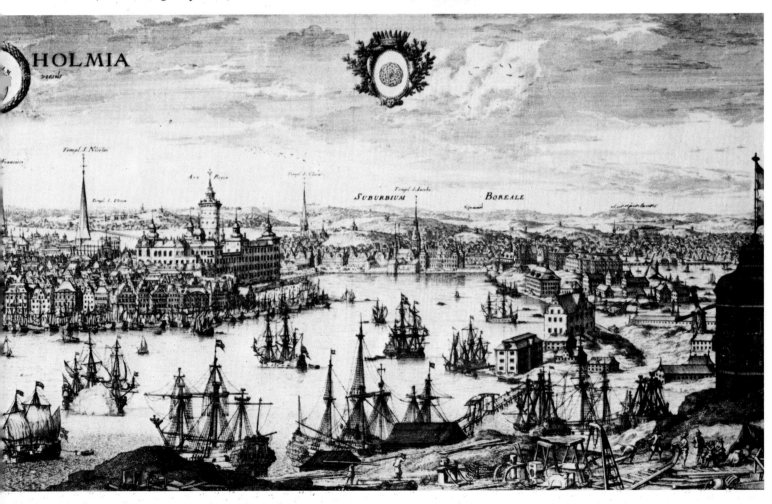

An engagement at Barösund in 1789 between Swedish and Russian fleets, and with forts ashore. By J T Schoultz. *Nationalmuseum, Stockholm.*

Swedish and Russian fleets engaging in 1789, with a Russian ship exploding (left of centre). By J T Schoultz. *Statens Sjöhistoriska Museum, Stockholm.*

fully evaded the Russians opposing him, though the King had a narrow escape from capture, the ship which was chasing him being recalled at the critical moment. As it was, Gustavus was able to reach Svensksund, south of Fredrikshamn, and to join a force which was already there.

It was the Prince of Nassau-Siegen, by a precipitate attack, made on 9 July in unfavourable weather in the hope of a resounding success to mark the Empress' birthday, who gave Gustavus the chance to turn the tables. Gustavus had drawn up his force in a strong position behind the low rocks of Svensksund Fjord, and when the Russians came on in reckless and disorderly fashion, he met them with such deadly fire that 9,500 of the enemy were killed, wounded or captured, and the Russian fleet almost destroyed. Swedish losses were fewer than 300. The Prince of Nassau-Siegen narrowly escaped capture, as Gustavus had done a few days earlier.

This was one of the proudest occasions in the history of the Swedish sailing and galley fleet, and Gustavus wisely took the opportunity to make an honourable peace. He had gained nothing by the war, and had it not been for his remarkable, if late, success, he could well have lost the whole of Finland.

Gustavus was the most discerning patron of artists. By good fortune there was a painter with his fleet, Johan Tietrich Schoultz (1754–1807) whose work, though practically unknown outside Sweden and Finland, deserves wider fame. Schoultz was in the tradition of the van de Veldes, father and son, who were not only official war artists on one side or the other during the earlier Anglo-Dutch maritime wars, but who also left records of the battle of the Sound.

Gustavus III was shot at a masked ball by one of his subjects, a tragic loss to his country. His son Gustavus IV had an unhappy life, for it was during his reign that Sweden became involved in the complicated war which between 1793 and 1815 enmeshed most of Europe and many territories beyond it.

The Swedish fleet played little direct part in this conflict, and at one stage the Baltic was controlled, during the ice-free months, by a British fleet under Sir James Saumarez. He proved a good friend to the country with which his own was allied for much of the tenure of his command, which was exercised from an anchorage off Gothenburg. But during the course of the European conflict Tsar Alexander I, when temporarily allied with Napoleon Bonaparte, took the chance to invade, conquer and annex Finland. For this misfortune Gustavus was blamed. He went into exile, and his throne was taken over, after the death of his uncle, the Duke of Södermanland, by the French marshal Bernadotte, much to the long-term advantage of the country.

As Denmark, which was twice attacked by a British fleet (once in 1801, when Nelson took part, and again in 1807 when the future Duke of

right
A model of the Swedish
Bellona class frigate built
in 1782.
*Statens Sjöhistoriska
Museum, Stockholm.*

below
Model of a Swedish galley
of 1749 fitted with lateen
sails.
*Statens Sjöhistoriska
Museum, Stockholm.*

left
A model of the Swedish ship of the line *Gustav IV Adolf*, built in the late eighteenth century. *Statens Sjöhistoriska Museum, Stockholm.*

below
A model of an eighteenth-century Swedish frigate showing sail. *Statens Sjöhistoriska Museum, Stockholm.*

Wellington served with the land forces), loyally adhered to the losing cause of France, she lost Norway to Sweden when the affairs of the Continent were resettled. This compensated Sweden for the loss of Finland, but it was an unhappy dispensation. It came to an end in 1905, when Norway regained the independence she had enjoyed in the Middle Ages. Finland won her freedom after the Russian Revolution of 1917.

There was only one occasion during the course of the nineteenth century when a Swedish fleet might have played a significant part in the affairs of northern Europe. This was when Denmark was attacked by Bismarck's Prussia, and the duchies of Schleswig and Holstein were filched from the Danish crown. The chance was missed. Scandinavian as she was, Sweden had little love for Denmark, and she preferred to cling to her neutrality, as she has since done with complete success. As, today, she still maintains one of the best-equipped among smaller navies, adequately supported by air power, she may claim that it has been through strength that she has been respected.

Gustavus III had discovered how impossible it was to challenge successfully the powerful neighbour in the east. Later Swedish statesmen have never attempted to do so. Their fleet is for home protection, not for those foreign adventures which once seemed so full of promise, but which ended in disappointment.

Amphion.

opposite, top
The Swedish victory at Svensksund in 1790, with the King's frigate in the foreground. By J T Schoultz.
Statens Sjöhistoriska Museum, Stockholm.

opposite, bottom
Rejoicings at Stockholm in 1790 after the return of Gustavus III from his victory over the Russian fleet at Svensksund. By J T Schoultz.
Statens Sjöhistoriska Museum, Stockholm.

left
A nineteenth-century representation of Gustavus III's command frigate *Amphion*, built by af Chapman.
Statens Sjöhistoriska Museum, Stockholm.

below
Eighteenth-century Stockholm, with a view of the harbour and the shipyard (centre). By G F Martin.
Statens Sjöhistoriska Museum, Stockholm.

THE FLEET OF FRANCE

Two of the most divergent comments ever made about the nature and effect of conflict at sea came, respectively, from a German and a Frenchman. The German, Ludwig Dehio, wrote: 'It is the peculiar characteristic of naval warfare that it compresses into days and hours crises which on land may be spun out over decades.' Dehio was considering the operation of the balance of power, and how it could be affected by a single major battle.

The occasion of the Frenchman's remark was both strange and significant, though it was not realised at the time. It was made in 1778 when Admiral Sir George Rodney was in Paris, kept there by his debts. The British government had invited him to return home, since they were hard pressed to find someone suitable for high command in North America. One of Rodney's friends, Marshal Biron, offered to lend him money in order to enable him to take up the offer. Before doing so, the Marshal thought he ought to clear the matter with the Minister of Marine, otherwise he might have been considered to be helping a hostile country. The Minister concerned, M. de Maurepas, was instantly reassuring. He said he thought nothing whatever of the effects of sea battles. 'It's just piff-poff on one side and t'other, and afterwards the sea looks just the same.'

The remark was ludicrous, coming from a man who was responsible for the navy of Louis XVI. Yet it was typical of an attitude to sea power which can be discerned almost throughout French history. Ever since her government became highly centralised, France had considered herself primarily as a land power, her navy being subsidiary to her army in the view of most of those who mattered.

Ironically it was the naval power of France, exercised during the American War of Independence, which ensured the success of the American rebels and thus significantly altered the balance of world power.

The more extreme political thinkers in France hailed the result with delight, and were encouraged by American success in their efforts to undermine the *ancien régime* in their own country.

The navy which in this unexpected way did so much to ensure a promising future for the United States was one of the best of its era. The French, together with the Dutch, had set standards in shipbuilding which had been widely followed. France had also produced the leading exponents of the art of sea warfare. The father of naval tactical studies was Paul Hoste (1652–1700), a Jesuit and Professor of Mathematics at the Royal College of the Marine at Toulon. His actual sea experience had been considerable, and his folio of 1697, *L'Art des Armées Navales,* was a seminal work studied in many countries, although it did not appear in English for nearly a century, the translation being made, significantly, by an enterprising junior officer, Lieutenant Christopher O'Bryen, who called it *Naval Evolutions.* Hoste, as his original title implied, thought in military terms. His 'art' was expressed in plans for outmanoeuvring an opponent and thus not being defeated at sea, rather than in recipes for victories. Hoste had noteworthy successors, including, in the nineteenth century, Pierre Bouguer, Vicomte de Morogues, who stressed the value of a systematic scheme of signals, and Bourdé de Villeheut, who wrote not long before the American War of Independence.

These writers inherited a tradition of French prowess at sea which went back to the days of galley warfare. Some of the most ornate and beautiful galleys ever built were French. The most widely known was *La Réale* of 1680. She was a successor to a line of galleys, similar though less elaborate which, since 1526, had borne the same name, indicating that they were the King's. These royal galleys flew the flags of both the sovereign and the galley commander, as they did in Spain. The largest of the type might have as many as seven rowers at each thwart, and a working crew of over 450 men. The most famous artist who worked on the royal galleys was Pierre Puget, some of whose elegant carvings are preserved in Paris. The larger galleys carried two lateen sails with an extensive spread of canvas. They were heavily armed, and were designed for Mediterranean conditions. They were used extensively until the early years of the eighteenth century.

On the broad oceans, and particularly across

below
The elaborately decorated
stern of a model of the
flagship *Royal Louis*
(built in 1692), which was
presented to the young
Louis XV for his
instruction in 1720. The
model bore his name.
Musée de la Marine, Paris.

opposite page
Louis XIV (reigned
1643–1715) by Hyacinte
Rigaud.
Louvre, Paris.

the Atlantic, the French naturally depended on sail. They shared with the Dutch and English a constant and highly successful interloping in the West Indies and elsewhere. In the islands of the Caribbean the French established themselves very early, in defiance of Spain, and there they settled permanently, as did the English. The French bred a race of buccaneers who made themselves greatly feared, and with good reason. They were leaders in the irregular and brutal warfare which for centuries made the Spanish Main a hotly disputed area.

Although the founder of the French sailing navy is usually said to have been Jean-Baptiste Colbert (1619–1683), Colbert in fact inherited a fleet which had been built up by the great Cardinal Richelieu (1585–1642). When the Cardinal came to power in 1624, France did not have a single ship which could compare with the latest Dutch and British men-of-war, and the native shipbuilders lacked both the knowledge and the resources to create a fleet of any capability. Richelieu ordered five large ships and a number of smaller ones from Dutch yards. The finest of them, the *St Louis* of 1626, with two gun decks and mounting about 60 guns, served as the prototype for many built subsequently in France. By the time Charles I of England had ordered the three-decked *Sovereign of the Seas,* one of the splendours of her age, the French had trained enough skilled shipwrights to make a significant reply. This was the *Couronne.* The ship was nearly as large as the *Sovereign* but had only two gun decks, mounting 72 guns. The French had surmised correctly that the English ship was likely to be difficult to handle. The *Couronne* proved herself better under sail and she could fire more effectively. It was a different matter when the *Sovereign* had been rebuilt.

After Richelieu's death the French navy was allowed to decay until it was revived by Colbert. Although he had something on which to build, he was forced, as his predecessor had been, to order ships from Holland. Once encouraged, shipbuilding revived so quickly that by 1663 the French two- and three-decked vessels were the envy of other nations.

During a visit she paid to Spithead in 1672 the 74-gun ship *Superbe* excited great interest. She was broader in the beam than English ships of her size, and her guns were higher out of the water. Charles II ordered his chief designer, Sir Anthony Deane, to copy the *Superbe*'s beat features. He did so and produced the *Harwich,* of 70 guns, which was such a success that she was used as a model for nine other ships of the line. Samuel Pepys, who as Secretary of the Admiralty followed all such matters closely, observed that 'only ships broad enough were sturdy enough'. From that time onwards, when French and English were at war, French prizes were valued not merely as additions to the strength of the English navy, but for the practical lessons which could so often be learnt from them. When, in

98

Designs by Pierre Puget
for the embellishment of
the ornate and beautiful
galley *La Réale*, built in
1680.
Musée de la Marine, Paris.

their turn, the French captured English ships, they nearly always reduced the number of guns, to make them better in a seaway. In justice to Sir Anthony Deane, it is fair to remember that he designed yachts so skilfully that within three years of the visit of the *Superbe* he was building them for Louis XIV.

In another respect, that of ordnance, the French navy as reorganised by Colbert introduced innovations which were destined to last. Among them was the mortar, adapted from the military variety. This was used to great effect for purposes of bombardment by Abraham Du Quesne, notable as one of the few admirals who ever got the better of de Ruyter.

The mortars fired bombs of 200 pounds with a high trajectory. They were particularly useful at a time when the projectiles used in the largest guns were of a mere 48 pounds. The mortars needed special ships. The obvious requirements were a broad beam, a steady platform and no foremast, so that the forward part of the vessel could be given over to the battery. The result was the 'bomb ketch', a familiar type for nearly a century and a half.

The life and career of Du Quesne, who made good use of the fleet which Colbert had revived, was full of ironies. He belonged to the Protestant faith in a predominantly Catholic country, and this factor, combined with an unusual arrogance, made him an unpopular figure in France. Much of his service had been abroad, and he was among the many officers who had learned some of their business in Sweden.

When Du Quesne clashed with de Ruyter both men were in their sixties and as Protestants their natural place would have been on the same side. But in 1676, at the time of the sea campaign off Sicily in which they were opposed, one of many changes of policy had allied Holland with Spain. De Ruyter's task was to prevent the relief of Messina, which was in the hands of rebels from Spanish rule who had called on France for help. He did so effectively for some time until April, when the French were sent reinforcements of such strength that they felt sufficiently confident to seek battle.

In an engagement off Augusta, de Ruyter, though he led the van, was not in chief command. This had been given to a Spaniard, Don Francisco de la Cerda, who placed his own squadron in the centre of the line. The other Dutch admiral, Haan, was thus prevented from supporting his fellow countryman, after the Spaniard had shown his ineptitude by not closing with the French. As a result, de Ruyter bore the brunt of Du Quesne's attack, and for the first time in his crowded life, he was hit by a shot. The Dutch and Spanish were forced to retreat, and later to relinquish their blockade of Sicily. De Ruyter, who was the admiration of friend and foe alike, died of his wounds at Syracuse on 29 April. Like that of Charles XII of Sweden, his death was worthy of a greater occasion, as even Colbert admitted.

left
Kronborg Castle,
Elsinore, as it is today.

below
The Swedish and Russian
fleets engage at the
second battle of
Svensksund in 1790. By
J T Schoultz.
*Nationalmuseum,
Stockholm.*

A view by Johan Tietrich Schoultz, a Swedish naval war artist, of the first battle of Svensksund, in August 1789, between the Swedes and Russians. *National Museum, Stockholm.*

below
Admiral Comte de Grasse (1722–1788), whose
operations at Chesapeake Bay led to the surrender of
Cornwallis and to the success of the Americans
ashore.
Musée de la Marine, Paris.

bottom
The port of Toulon, one of a series of large-scale
views of French ports by Claude Joseph Vernet
(1714–1789).
Musée de la Marine, Paris.

below
The ornamental stern of the *Soleil Royal*, which was
burnt off Cherbourg in 1692 after an attack by the
English *Sovereign of the Seas*.
Bibliothèque Nationale, Paris.

Many chroniclers of the French navy consider
that among its most notable feats was the delaying action fought off Barfleur in 1692 by de Tourville, who had a success against the English and
Dutch off Beachy Head two years earlier. This
was during what is sometimes known as the War
of the English Succession, since one of the many
aims of the French was to oust William of Orange
from the throne of England, and to restore the
Catholic James II, who had fled the country in
1688.

De Tourville was certainly a gallant man.
Faced by a combined fleet of a hundred ships,
with only 44 of his own, he fought brilliantly
before being forced to withdraw. His fleet was
then split up. De Tourville's own flagship, the
Soleil Royal, was overwhelmed and burnt off
Cherbourg after an attack by the *Sovereign of the
Seas,* which had been built by Charles I. Sir
George Rooke added to the destruction at the
battle of la Hogue.

The French navy met with a series of reverses
during the Seven Years War (1756–1762), during
the course of which Canada was lost along with
various West Indian islands, including Martini-
que, which fell to a combined expedition led by
Rodney and Monckton. Britain gained a firmer
position in India, and when Spain joined France
she suffered the humiliation of a British occupation of Manila. So firmly has the history of the
Philippines since been linked with that of the
United States that many historians find the fact
hard to credit.

The events of this war led the French to a
natural wish for revenge. The opportunity
occurred during and after 1778, when the British
had their hands fully occupied in America and
elsewhere. The chance was eagerly taken, all the

more so since France had evidence that many Englishmen sympathised with their kinsfolk across the Atlantic. Their judgement was right. Even the British navy was soon torn by dissension, which came to a head in the recriminations following an inconclusive action fought in the Atlantic between Keppel and d'Orvilliers.

At one stage a large combined Franco-Spanish fleet dominated the Channel, and might have successfully supported an invasion had it been handled with more decision. As crisis followed crisis, the Admiralty in London were hard put to it to fill the principal commands, hence their request to Rodney, who had made a name for himself in the earlier war. Rodney suffered from constant ill health, but he distinguished his return to active service with two major successes. During the winter season of 1780 he convoyed supplies to Gibraltar, which was then enduring the longest of its various sieges. In the course of the operation he encountered a Spanish force under Admiral de Langara, and in a moonlight battle near Cape St Vincent destroyed the greater part of it without loss to himself. Then he sailed for the West Indies, where, during the next few seasons, he was to be engaged in a strategic duel with first de Guichen and later the Comte de Grasse.

The duty of the Frenchmen was to guard their country's Caribbean possessions, and to threaten the British operating in support of the army in North America. Rodney's duty was to counter both these aims. The resultant actions and brushes were inconclusive, and it was not until the later months of 1781, when Rodney was in England on leave of absence, that the battle occurred which had so momentous a consequence. In itself, it was one of those 'piff-poff' affairs, to borrow the phrase of M. de Maurepas, which so often recurred in sail warfare. Afterwards the sea was indeed the same, but ashore it was very different.

It was at a time when the British general Cornwallis was advancing through Carolina and Virginia, in the expectation that at Hampton Roads he would receive the essential supplies which would enable him to continue his campaign. Five days after a British squadron under Hood had left the anchorage, believing the French to be further north, de Grasse arrived at the Capes of Virginia and anchored, without opposition, inside Cape Henry. There he disembarked troops, conferred with Washington, the American commander, and sent ships to blockade the rivers James and York. The British army, thus invested, shut itself up in Yorktown.

right
Louis Antoine de
Bougainville (1729–1811),
soldier, diplomat,
mathematician, admiral
and circumnavigator.

below
A view of the port of
Marseilles. By C J Vernet.
Musée de la Marine, Paris.

Admiral Graves, the senior British naval officer in Rodney's absence, was quite unaware of de Grasse's movements, and believed him to be somewhere off Cuba. When Hood joined him, he had a force of twenty ships, and his obvious course was to sail to help Cornwallis. With the wind behind him, Graves approached the entrance to the Chesapeake, fully expecting to reassure the army.

On the morning of 5 September 1781 the French were alerted by their watching frigates, which hastened to the anchorage to report Graves' presence. De Grasse ordered his captains to slip their cables. He had no wish to be attacked while at anchor, or when beating about in confined waters. He made for the open sea, and as his flagship, the *Ville de Paris,* the largest vessel of her time, rounded Cape Henry as the eleventh in the French line, it was to find that Graves was in the process of ranging his ships according to the time-hallowed Fighting Instructions. Graves was later to complain that his captains showed a lack of initiative, but if he had signalled 'General Chase', as a bolder man might have done, he

would almost certainly have destroyed the French piecemeal.

Bougainville, at the head of the French van, veered away instead of continuing to tack into the wind. This was a correct procedure, for it had the effect of delaying the general action and gave time for de Grasse to deploy his ships in an orderly fashion.

It was four in the afternoon before a general bombardment began. When it did so, the British suffered more damage than the French, and one ship, the *Terrible,* was handled so severely that she later became a total loss. Although he had the advantage of the wind, and thus could enforce as much or as little action as he wished, Graves gradually drew off. For five whole days the two fleets manoeuvred within sight of each other. Then came a shift of wind, and de Grasse, who was expecting reinforcements and had taken the measure of his opponent, returned to his anchorage, secure in the knowledge that he would not be attacked. The British would need to repair their ships, and would go north to do so. This was exactly what Graves did.

The whole strategic picture had been altered in favour of the French and Americans. Washington and Rochambeau, at the head of the French contingent ashore, tightened their grip on Yorktown, and Cornwallis had no choice but to

capitulate. This he did on 19 October, within a few weeks of the battle.

Washington was fully aware of what his fellow-countrymen owed to French sea power. 'In any operation', he wrote, 'and under all circumstances, a decisive naval superiority is to be considered as a fundamental principle, and the basis upon which every hope of success must ultimately depend.' He had found such a basis, and a wave of rejoicing was felt throughout America. The end of the war was to be delayed, but it was in sight.

De Grasse was as experienced a seaman as his navy then possessed. He was born in 1722, the same year as de Suffren, who was the greatest tactician of his era. Both men served for a time with the fleet of the Knights of Malta, as did de Tourville before them. De Suffren's most significant engagements were in the Far East, where he fought a series of actions with Sir Edward Hughes to try to gain mastery in Indian waters. De Grasse had had his great moment; so had Bougainville, the most famous of his captains, who had fought his ship with great distinction. He had already won renown for a circumnavigation he had achieved, earlier in the century, at a time when James Cook, on behalf of Britain, was mapping the Pacific.

When Rodney returned to his command to face

right
A French lieutenant of 1793.
Musée de la Marine, Paris.

far right
A French sailor of 1793.
Musée de la Marine, Paris.

de Grasse, a very different spirit prevailed than had been apparent under Graves. The adversaries met on 12 April 1782 in the Saints Passage off the island of Dominica. They were fairly matched, but Rodney's gunnery was better, and at a critical stage in the battle a shift of wind enabled the British to pierce the French line and to capture, then and later, after a chase by Hood, eight ships. De Grasse himself surrendered in the *Ville de Paris*.

The encounter saved Jamaica from invasion, and it brought Rodney a well-deserved peerage, though at the time of the event an order recalling him was on its way westward. Rodney duly returned home, and although he himself saw no further active service, his victory, belated as it was, enabled his country to make a better peace than would otherwise have been the case. The *Ville de Paris* was lost in a great storm on her way back to England, but de Grasse survived.

At the time of the French admiral's death in 1788, the French navy was at the summit of its glory, for not only had the main fleet fulfilled every reasonable expectation, but in the sphere of commerce raiding, in which French captains had long excelled, it had proved a thorn in the side of its enemy. The French privateers were also feared, for theirs was a type of warfare well suited to daring and enterprising spirits.

A bust commemorating the great French tactician de Suffren (1726–1788). By Jean-Antoine Houdon. *Musée de la Marine, Paris.*

below
A model of de Grasse's flagship *Ville de Paris*, the largest vessel of her time, which was captured by Rodney at the battle of the Saints in 1782. *US Naval Academy Museum, Annapolis, Maryland.*

VILLARET DE JOYEUSE.

When Revolution broke upon the country, the navy suffered greatly, far more so than the army, which was turned into a citizen force which was soon dreaded throughout Europe. The long-established and necessarily closed system which prevailed in the sea service was discarded too hastily, since it took time to train young officers, however zealous, for the responsibilities of commanding fleets. Nevertheless, much was done, even within a short time, as was shown by the first major battle of a war at sea which was to continue, with one breathing space, from 1792 to 1815.

The occasion was the early summer of 1794, and the protagonists were Lord Howe and Admiral Villaret-Joyeuse. A greater contrast than that between the two men could scarcely be imagined. Howe was an aristocrat by birth who had given his long life to the study of his profession and had held important commands in three separate wars. Villaret-Joyeuse was just over forty and had been propelled to the top by the elimination of his seniors. With him sailed what would now be called a political commissar, Jean Bon St André, who knew nothing of naval tactics but who, by his revolutionary enthusiasm, had infused new life into the base at Brest.

Howe was at sea to guard outward and inward convoys, and also with the hope of meeting the French fleet. Villaret-Joyeuse's task was simpler. It was to ensure that essential grain supplies reached France from America. Both men may be held to have succeeded in their aims, for although Howe defeated the French on 1 June and captured six ships, Villaret-Joyeuse safeguarded the grain. He had also shown that the navy of the Revolution could fight as gallantly as its predecessors and that it could not only send large fleets to sea, but maintain them there as long as necessary, a fact which some had doubted.

Although it was the French army upon which the main burden of war fell, the navy in 1798 was able to land an army of 40,000 men in Egypt. The threat of a cross-channel invasion occupied a high proportion of British resources, and when Spain joined France in a temporary and uneasy alliance, their combined fleet presented a formidable threat. Nelson defeated it at Trafalgar; even so, there were ten more years of struggle, during the course of which British sea commerce needed constant protection. If France, despite the genius of Bonaparte, was in the end defeated, it was not entirely because the seas were controlled by her enemies.

In the course of history, no nation has shown greater or quicker powers of recovery than France, and her navy was no exception. So much was this so that within twelve years of the ending of the Napoleonic Wars, a French squadron was engaged in the last notable action fought wholly under sail. This was in 1827, in the Bay of Navarino. There a combined fleet of British, French and Russians destroyed a Turkish-Egyptian force at anchor, during the course of the war for the liberation of Greece. The Commander-in-Chief, Sir Edward Codrington, a veteran of Trafalgar, was held to have exceeded his orders, in that war had not formally been declared. In contrast, the French admiral, de Rigny, was received with acclaim on his return home. This was the first time since the seventeenth century that French and British captains had fought on the same side.

They did so again during the Crimean War. By then, although by outward appearances ships of the line resembled their stately forerunners, steam had become a factor in naval warfare, and was soon to dominate it. The French had already employed it on active service, for in 1838 Admiral Baudin made a successful attack on the fortress at San Juan d'Ulloa, after French property had suffered from a mutiny in the Mexican army. Steam tugs were employed to tow bombardment ships into position, and explosive shot of a kind devised by the French general Poixhans ensured the surrender of the Mexicans involved, and the satisfaction of just claims. The action was observed by an American officer, the future Admiral Farragut, the principal Federal commander during the American Civil War, who sent a valuable report to his superiors.

left
A model of the armoured
ship *Hoche*, of 1880,
showing her anti-torpedo
nets.
Musée de la Marine, Paris.

below
The armoured steam
frigate *Gloire* of 1859.
By François Roux.
Musée de la Marine, Paris.

A coal-burning destroyer of the time of the First World War.

The heavily armed ship *Suffren* of 1899, which served in the First World War.

The French battleship *Bouvet*, sunk during an attack at the Dardanelles in 1915.

French constructors, always advanced, made a great step forward towards the modern ship-of-war in 1859, when Dupuy de Lome produced the armoured frigate *Gloire*. Although she had a wooden hull, her vitals were protected by heavy plating, and powerful engines gave her a good turn of speed. The British replied with the *Warrior*, built wholly of iron, with armour amidships.

The French navy was involved in minor wars and incidents in various parts of the world during the later nineteenth century. The most memorable of these took place in what became known as Indo-China, much of which has since been the object of stern dispute under the name of Vietnam. A treaty signed in June 1880 recognised a French protectorate, but it was the sustained efforts of Admiral Courbet in defeating a Chinese force at Foochow in August 1884 which made his country's aspirations a reality. Courbet was expert in handling a new weapon in sea warfare, the torpedo. By later standards his equipment was primitive, but the Chinese soon discovered how effective it could be.

France relied upon Britain to sustain the main burden at sea during the First World War, but her own contribution was never negligible. On occasion, as during the Dardanelles campaign, it could be spectacular. The conduct of Admiral Guépratte in the naval attack on the Turkish forts in March 1915 was universally admired. The four French battleships which took part were met with an appalling fire, and the *Bouvet*, travelling fast in Eren Keui Bay, was suddenly rocked by a great explosion. She heeled over and capsized in a cloud of smoke and steam, with the loss of almost all her complement. The episode was as dramatic as anything which took place during that disastrous campaign, when French and British sailors once more fought side by side.

Between the two World Wars, French naval architects showed that they had lost none of their traditional skill and ingenuity. This was particularly apparent in the submarine arm. France had devoted an increasing proportion of her naval budget to the submarine ever since the days in the 1890s when Max Laubeuf devised a highly advanced type of hull. In 1929 she produced, in the *Surcouf,* named after a famous privateer of the Napoleonic era, one of the largest and most complex submarines ever launched. Her length was 361 feet and she was given two 8-inch guns as well as ten torpedo tubes. She also carried an aircraft in a special hangar, and seemed to most experts to have every requirement for commerce raiding. She was sunk on war service in 1942.

In other directions, French design was advanced. There was for instance *Le Terrible,* a destroyer of 1922 with a maximum speed of $45\frac{1}{2}$ knots. At the time this seemed fantastic, even for a short burst. There were two fast and well-armed battle-cruisers, the *Dunkerque* and the *Strasbourg,* and the aircraft carrier *Béarn,* which was far less cumbersome in appearance than most of her contemporaries.

French and British squadrons were once more ranged on the same side during the opening phases of the Second World War. Then came the massive German advance by land in the summer months of 1940. Although the French army was defeated, her navy remained intact. Much of it was immobilised, and an attack by the British on the base at Oran, in order to prevent important units falling into enemy hands, was an incident which led to considerable bitterness.

France took heart under General de Gaulle, her inspiration in time of trouble, and her navy was represented in some of the later phases of the war in the Far East against Japan. Her ships included the new battleship *Richelieu,* named after the founder of the French navy. The splendid appearance of this vessel, which embodied many of the latest refinements in surface weapons, was an appropriate symbol of the revival of a great fighting Service.

The French armoured cruiser *Bruix* at Salonika in 1915 during the First World War. Her formidable ram is noteworthy.

The Free French ship *Le Terrible*, capable of very high speed, which served with the Allies in the Second World War.

The large French submarine *Surcouf*, which served in the Second World War until she was sunk in 1942.

NELSON'S FLEET

Samuel Pepys, famed as a diarist, and perhaps the ablest Secretary of the Admiralty in London ever to have taken office, once wrote of the qualities to be looked for in an efficient fleet. Integrity and specialised knowledge were not enough. There must be vigour, assiduity, affection, strictness of discipline, method. The strenuous conjunction of zeal, honesty, good husbandry and technical excellence were, he felt sure, the proper foundation on which to build. It sounded a counsel of perfection, and in a sense it was. Nevertheless, there was a stage in the history of the navy which Pepys had once served when it could be said with truth that it possessed most of the attributes he thought were necessary, some of them to a high degree.

This happy state of affairs came about at the time when Horatio Nelson was developing his full powers as a leader of men. The fleet he commanded at Trafalgar in 1805 has been regarded as the best expression of the great era of sail. This is a fair judgement, with the proviso that a heterogeneous body of men, drawn from every layer of society, serving in a collection of ships of extremely varying ages, some of them prizes, is likely to be a long way from perfection.

There were two ingredients not stressed by Pepys which gave Nelson's fleet a special quality and made it dreaded by its opponents. It embodied more war experience than had ever before been assembled, endured under an astonishing variety of conditions and in most parts of the world. Furthermore it was given strength by officers and men who had been more continually afloat, in all weathers and at all seasons of the year, than any other fleet of its time. In these respects, few predecessors could rival it and none of them could surpass it. If the word 'invincible' is ever justified, this was where it could have been applied.

There were excellent reasons why Nelson himself was looked upon by his American biographer, Alfred Thayer Mahan, as 'the embodiment of sea power'. When the Admiral was a child, Britain rejoiced at the events of the 'Wonderful Year' 1759, when by land and sea her arms were victorious. He was just over a year old when Hawke, in a bold and dramatic chase,

fought Conflans among the rocks and shoals of Quiberon Bay, and destroyed the *Soleil Royal*, successor to the flagship lost by de Tourville. Hawke's most notable captain was Lord Howe, who as a midshipman had sailed under Anson in the opening stages of his voyage of circumnavigation of 1740–44 and who later ruled at the Admiralty and gave Nelson his one and only peace-time command. Hawke himself, the exemplar of vigorous tactics, survived to see Nelson's name on the list of post-captains.

Nelson's sea experience was enviably wide and varied. He had served as a boy on board a merchantman in the West Indies. Like Drake, he had learnt pilotage in the Thames estuary. He had been on an expedition to the Arctic and had served for some time in the Far East; he had fought on land in Nicaragua and Corsica and he knew the waters of the Channel, the North Sea, the Mediterranean and the Atlantic, as well as most seamen of his time.

Before he was given his supreme opportunity against the combined French and Spanish fleets at Trafalgar, he had been in action over a hundred times, including a number of major fleet actions. Of these, the most notable had been Lord St Vincent's engagement with the Spaniards in February 1797 when Nelson, who was then a commodore, had by his personal initiative ensured the interception of part of the opposing fleet. The following year he had been given command of a detached squadron and with it he had annihilated a French fleet at the battle of the Nile. In 1801, as second in command under Sir Hyde Parker, he had borne the whole brunt of the attack made on the fleet of Denmark, and by his disregard of a pusillanimous signal, had ensured the success of a most difficult assignment.

Stiff assignments were common form in Nelson's time, for although the fleet, as a fleet, was never defeated, its commitments were worldwide and it was constantly overstretched. Technically, in their construction and equipment, the ships were ultra-conservative, a traditional fault with the British. Those in charge relied for predominance on what Mahan called 'combat superiority', that is, on the *habit* of winning. It was the result of discipline, training, sheer hard

121

work and protracted endurance. Officers and men often envied the ships they fought, for the French, who encouraged ideas and forward-looking skills, had lost none of their prowess in shipbuilding. Even the Spaniards, sadly declined as they had become, still produced ships which Nelson's friend and colleague, Collingwood, once described as 'beauties'.

Every senior officer in the Trafalgar fleet had been brought up in a school of adversity, for as younger men they had had to digest the painful lessons of the American War of Independence, when the Navy had been overtaxed and could not prevent humiliation ashore. Nelson had not been immune. The campaign against the Spaniards in Nicaragua in which he had taken part had been a failure. He had been invalided home, and had been given a passage in HMS *Lion* by Captain Cornwallis. The two men became friends and Nelson learnt much from the officer affectionately known as 'Billy Blue'. Cornwallis had been one of Rodney's captains at his victory over de Grasse. For much of the Napoleonic War, he was in command of the powerful western squadron, the main British fleet, whose duty was to guard the approaches to the Channel, with all incoming and outgoing convoys. This was the hinge of British sea strategy.

Adversity had taught the fleet to respect opponents, though not to overrate them. Admirals and captains were not unduly depressed by failure. Like his fellows, Nelson himself had learned the hard way, through a succession of reverses which extended almost throughout his career alongside his triumphs. Towards the close of the American war, he had attempted to capture Turks Island in the West Indies from the French garrison, and had been driven off. In the war with France of which the Trafalgar campaign was part, he had seen Lord Hood driven from Toulon. Later he had lost the use of his right eye at Calvi in Corsica, and his right arm in a foiled attempt on Tenerife. Even after his victories at the Nile and Copenhagen he failed in an attack on the well-defended harbour at Boulogne, where Napoleon had assembled barges for the invasion of Britain which he had long had in mind. It could never be said of Nelson, as was written on Hawke's monument, that 'where'er he sailed, Victory attended him'. It did not. Nelson worked hard for it and sometimes it eluded him.

The men of Nelson's fleet were, for the most part, strange material. An essential nucleus of experienced seamen was reinforced by a crowd of pressed men, not all of them bred to the sea. There were jail birds, undesirables of all kinds and exiles drawn from many countries, including America and France. Discipline, like the life in general, was harsh. Samuel Johnson was not far wrong when he remarked to Boswell that 'being in a ship is being in a jail, with the chance of being drowned'. He had himself seen and been shocked by conditions on board a man-of-war, when he had spent some days as the guest of a naval officer. He added: 'a man in a jail has more room, better food, and commonly better company'. Johnson was right about the room, but the average prisoner of his time did not eat as well

Admiral Lord Hawke
(1705–1781), exemplar of
valour and tenacity,
victor at Quiberon Bay
in 1759. He later became
First Lord of the
Admiralty. By Francis
Cotes.
*National Maritime
Museum, Greenwich.
(Greenwich Hospital
Collection).*

as the sailor, or get a generous allowance of drink, and as for company, whatever the material may have been to start with, good officers very quickly produced good men.

Except for admirals and captains, the lives of the officers were fairly spartan. What united them was the fact that they were professional to a degree unknown in many other walks of life. They spoke a language of their own and they lived in a strange, unpredictable element, in which a constant factor was danger. Nelson used to speak affectionately of 'Children of the Service' and it was true that the Navy was largely hereditary. There were dining clubs where captains met in London, and where they discussed their problems and aired their grievances, of which there were usually plenty. To be elected was no formality. The first club of its kind had been started in Pepys' time, and its originators were eleven flag officers and captains, each one of whom had been prominent in the wars against the Dutch. Nelson belonged to two. One of them dated from when he was a child, the other from the period of the American War. They have since been united as the 'Royal Navy Club of 1765 and 1785'. Nelson, tactical innovator that he was, believed in working with, not against his fellows. How fully they accepted him is shown by the fact that he was readily listened to, even by his seniors. How loyal he was, and remained, to anyone with whom he had served is apparent from his letters. He was even loyal to Sir Hyde Parker, whose ineptitude had so nearly led to disaster at Copenhagen. Nelson supplanted him, but not through intrigue. The Admiralty ordered it, doubtless realising that he should have had the chief command in the first place.

Nelson's loyalty extended to ships, particularly to those in which he had served. This was most notable in the case of the *Agamemnon*, a

64-gun ship built in 1781 at Buckler's Hard, on the Beaulieu river in Hampshire, and twelve years old when he first trod her quarter-deck. He operated this ship in the Mediterranean until she was almost falling to pieces. He would not exchange her when offered a bigger and newer vessel and only transferred when the *Agamemnon* was no longer capable of the duties expected of her. It was later his pleasure to find her in Parker's fleet bound for the Baltic, though she grounded just before the battle of Copenhagen and took no part in it. But under Sir Edward Berry, whose career had been made by Nelson, she was present at Trafalgar and had a narrow escape from capture on her way to join the fleet.

As for the *Victory*, this great three-decker was Nelson's stately home for years on end, during the watch on Toulon which engaged him from 1802 onwards. She has survived to this day as a memorial to those who sailed in her. She was launched in 1765, shortly after the conclusion of the Seven Years War, and was thus forty years old at Trafalgar. But she had been twice rebuilt, and besides being powerfully armed, with 100 guns and two carronades for close fighting, she was an exceptional sailer, the best of her size in the fleet except possibly for Collingwood's flagship, the *Royal Sovereign,* which had been lately docked and recoppered and thus transformed from being a sluggard.

It so happened that during the course of her active life the *Victory* flew the flag of a succession of admirals who either helped to bring Nelson's fleet to its peak at Trafalgar, or helped to maintain its influence on world affairs immediately afterwards. They included Richard Kempenfelt, Lord Howe, Lord Hood, Lord St Vincent and Sir James Saumarez. All these officers except the first were well acquainted with Nelson and some were close friends.

opposite, top
John Jervis, later Earl of St Vincent (1735–1825), as a young man. Victor against the Spaniards in 1797, St Vincent later became First Lord of the Admiralty. By Francis Cotes. *National Portrait Gallery, London.*

opposite, bottom
Admiral Rodney's victory off Dominica, where he beat the Comte de Grasse, on 12 April 1782. Seen here is the attack on the French flagship *Ville de Paris.* By J C Schetky.

left
Captain the Hon William Cornwallis, later admiral and Commander-in-Chief (1744–1819), an early friend of Nelson. Portrait in gouache and pastel, hitherto unpublished. By Daniel Gardner. *Private Collection.*

below
Portsmouth Dockyard in 1790. By Robert Dodd. *National Maritime Museum, Greenwich.*

above
A scene on the quarter-deck of Howe's flagship, the *Queen Charlotte*, on the 'Glorious' First of June. On the left stands Lord Howe, with sword drawn; near by, Captain Neville of the Queen's Regiment lies mortally wounded in the arms of friends; while on the right the Captain of the ship, Sir Andrew Snape Douglas, wilts slightly from a head wound.
British Museum, London

right
The battle of the First of June, 1794. The French *Vengeur* (left centre) sinks after her duel with the *Brunswick*. By Robert Dodd.
National Maritime Museum, Greenwich.

It was mainly to Kempenfelt and Howe that the fleet owed an extension of the signal system, whose former limitations had once so inhibited tactics. Kempenfelt, the son of an army officer who had been in Marlborough's wars, came of an aristocratic Swedish family of great distinction. He was the most thoughtful officer of his time. Having little 'influence', his promotion was slow, but he had been flag captain and chief of staff to Admiral Cornish at the capture of Manila during the Seven Years War. A charming picture by Tilly Kettle shows him with the admiral and his secretary in the great cabin of the *Norfolk,* obviously discussing operational plans in that intimate way which shipboard life necessarily encouraged.

As a junior rear-admiral Kempenfelt served in Howe's fleet. In a brilliant action during the winter of 1781 against de Guichen he showed how a small force, by bold and skilful tactics, could outwit a superior force and capture a valuable convoy from under its very nose. Within a few months, when preparing for the relief of Gibraltar, Kempenfelt went down in the *Royal George* off Spithead, whilst the ship was heeled for a small repair. He was a great loss to the nation and the navy, but by the time of his death many of his ideas were in practical use.

Although he never served under Lord Howe in battle, Nelson had the highest regard for this most experienced admiral and administrator. Howe wrote to Nelson to express astonishment

above
Horatio, Viscount Nelson (1758–1805), the well-known portrait of 1798 by L F Abbot showing Nelson wearing the Order of the Bath. *National Portrait Gallery, London.*

above
The clash at St Vincent showing (centre) a Spanish ship attacked by the *Captain*, flying Nelson's pennant as a Commodore. By Sir William Allan.
National Maritime Museum, Greenwich (Greenwich Hospital Collection).

right
Nelson leading a boarding party to the Spanish *San Josef* at the battle off St Vincent, 1797. By George Jones.
National Maritime Museum, Greenwich (Greenwich Hospital Collection)

opposite, top
Engraving after Isaac Cruickshank of the Seamen's Delegates during the Mutiny of the Nore, 1797.
National Maritime Museum, Greenwich.

opposite, bottom
The approach of Nelson's ships (top right) towards the French line at the Battle of the Nile, 1798. By Nicholas Pocock.
National Maritime Museum, Greenwich.

The blowing up of the French flagship *L'Orient* at the Nile, with British ships ranged on each side. By George Arnauld. *National Maritime Museum, Greenwich (Greenwich Hospital Collection).*

that all the captains had supported him so well at the Nile. His own career had at times been chequered because subordinates did not always understand him as well as they should have done. There had been no 'uniformity of zeal' such as Nelson seemed able to inspire. This was the new spirit, welcome, and to Howe at least, surprising.

Nelson's admiration for Lord Hood was not widely shared by his contemporaries, especially among those who knew him best. He had done well under Rodney during the American War but his lack of enterprise at the Chesapeake had been remarked. Hood was a biting critic of others, and army officers with the task of co-operating with him, as in Corsica, found him arrogant, which was probably a correct judgement. But he had great faith in Nelson, whom he employed on various missions in the Mediterranean when, at the outbreak of war in 1793, he was appointed to that station.

As for Lord St Vincent, who had fought in the *Victory* at the battle of 1797 which had brought him his earldom, there was a man after Nelson's heart. St Vincent possessed every characteristic that would have appealed to the ardent and ambitious. He had made his own way upwards, and had the good fortune to serve under Saunders in the expedition to Quebec in 1759 which had given Wolfe immortality and added a great country to the British crown. In the Mediterranean, St Vincent had given Nelson almost a free hand, and had approved his boldness in turning out of the line during his famous battle in order to prevent the escape of Spanish ships.

It had been St Vincent who had detached Nelson to go in search of the French expedition to Egypt and thus given him the chance to destroy Brueys' squadron. And it was St Vincent who, as head of the Admiralty, had replaced Parker in the Baltic and put Nelson in his place. The fleet itself owed much to St Vincent's ruthless discipline. Officers and men chafed at this, and complained behind his back, but he turned the fleet into a splendid instrument of war. 'No man in England', wrote Collingwood, 'is more capable of conducting the Naval department than he is'. That was true, although while Howe lived, it was to him that St Vincent turned as a pattern. 'Lord Howe always wore blue breeches', he used to say, 'and I like to follow him even in my dress'. After Howe's death, in 1799, it was in St Vincent that right-minded officers found inspiration, not least for his tenacity. Those who knew the formidable old man, savoured that vein of humour which could sometimes sweeten the sharpest command.

The last admiral to take the *Victory* on operational service was one of the rivals to Nelson in point of major fleet actions. Sir James Saumarez, who was almost Nelson's own age, had exchanged from a frigate to a ship of the line just before Rodney's battle off Dominica in 1782. He lived to become the last survivor of Rodney's captains on that memorable day. He had been knighted for a gallant frigate action in 1793, and had fought in the *Orion* under St Vincent when he beat the Spaniards. He was the senior captain under Nelson at the battle of the Nile, and although he missed Copenhagen and Trafalgar he had won his own victory off Algeçiras in 1801 after suffering an initial reverse from which less resolute men would have needed time to recover.

Saumarez's last and most important mission was at the head of a fleet which between 1808 and 1813 kept control of the Baltic during the ice-free months, and thus ensured a flow of trade to and from England, despite every effort of Napoleon and his allies to stop the flow. During the winters, when Saumarez was at home, the *Victory* was used to convey troops and supplies to Wellington in the Peninsula. It was a fitting end to her active career, before she was made guardship at Portsmouth, where she still remains.

In their time both Saumarez and Collingwood, Nelson's reliable friend and comrade-in-arms, had served under Cornwallis in the most dangerous employment of the British fleet. This was the close watch which was maintained on the French Atlantic port and base at Brest. The perils were not from the enemy but from rock, shoal, storm, freak of wind and strain on ships. Men wore themselves out on this unspectacular but essential duty, as they had done ever since the days of Hawke. Off Toulon, Nelson had kept distant watch. Off Brest, come what may, ships were closer in, and a stage was reached when, after months at sea, Collingwood remarked that the Admiralty had better invent a patent, mechanical admiral. Flesh and blood could stand so much and no more.

Battle was an immense relief and exhilaration, as well as a trial of nerve, to such officers as these. It was different for those they watched. Snug in port, the French could think of the British wearing themselves out, but when the wind came from the east and they were able to sail if they so wished, they seldom did so with the alacrity their Emperor expected. Who could blame them? The captains of the ships of the line had far too little practice in seamanship. In the main, it was the frigates, the privateers and small detached forces led by enterprising spirits who kept up morale.

Trafalgar was one of the rewards of patience, and the tactics of the battle have been argued endlessly, in the hope of extracting permanent lessons. Villeneuve, with his French and Spanish ships, had gone to Cadiz, after being chased by Nelson as far as the West Indies and being brought to inconclusive action by Calder on his return to Europe. He was some weeks in port before Napoleon ordered him to the Mediterranean, since French plans of invasion had been shelved. Villeneuve was reluctant to sail on what seemed likely to be a hopeless mission; as a survivor of the Nile he knew the capabilities of his opponent all too well. Napoleon despatched someone to replace him, and this unfeeling action spurred Villeneuve to put to sea.

Nelson had made a careful plan of attack, which was not only familiar to his captains but was almost public property; certainly the French knew about it. His original idea was to employ three lines, although in the upshot his resources did not allow this. When Villeneuve was fairly in the open, as he was by 20 October, Nelson felt so confident of success (his 27 ships were to face 33) that, although his scheme in the main was kept to, his captains, in the words of one of them, 'scrambled into action' as best they could. The entire battle was unorthodox, the two admirals, Nelson and Collingwood, leading their respective lines straight at the enemy. The result was that the *Victory* and the *Royal Sovereign* suffered far more severely than the ships that followed, Nelson being killed and Collingwood wounded. The price was paid, but matters went as Nelson had intended. Collingwood's line, as the plan had indicated, wrought havoc among the rear of Villeneuve's fleet, while Nelson prevented interference with the work of destruction and then helped to complete it.

Not many ships escaped, and of those that did, four were snapped up a fortnight later by Sir Richard Strachan. It was as thorough a victory as was possible in view of the storm which blew up afterwards and the inevitable damage to Nelson's ships, many of which lost their ground tackle and so could not anchor. Only four prizes reached Gibraltar, but the largest man-of-war in the world, the Spanish *Santissima Trinidada*, sank after heavy pounding, and thirteen other French and Spanish ships were wrecked, burnt, or sank under tow. Of the 33 vessels which had set out for the Mediterranean, only eleven returned to Cadiz, three of them after being recaptured from exhausted prize crews. Nelson's signal, made on the morning of 21 October, 'England expects that every man will do his duty', had been well and truly obeyed, and he could die content.

He worked by charm. Men did their best for him, and often better than they realised was in them. This was because he trusted them and took them into his confidence in all his plans, thus assuring them that their problems were taken into account. He praised them when they shone and gave everyone the fullest credit possible. Confidence, encouragement and personal charm worked miracles. Even when he failed, Nelson blamed nobody but himself. So rare and generous a spirit does not occur often and is most uncommon in high command. 'There is but one Nelson', wrote Lord St Vincent, and successors found how true the words were.

Nelson's belief in freedom had its reverse side, although in fact this did not matter. St Vincent once remarked that Nelson's own ships were disordered, though they fought splendidly; moreover, he was so far from observing the hallowed rules and instructions for formal tactics that his fleets never presented that regular appearance so desired by Rodney, Howe and others. Nelson

had his eye on essentials, and he was among the first to realise that the more scope an able man is given, the better he will do, provided he knows that his superior will back him up afterwards. Howe did not believe he had many able captains, and to have given them any measure of scope would, he thought, have been disastrous. He was a centraliser. Nelson's outlook was entirely the opposite, and although he was certainly lucky in the men he led, they would not have done so well under any other commander.

Nelson's successor, Collingwood, had exceptional virtues and the one serious shortcoming

The evening of the Battle of Trafalgar, painted by W J Huggins. *National Maritime Museum, Greenwich.*

right
Model of the shipyard at Buckler's Hard, Hampshire, in 1803 with the frigate *Euryalus* building.

below
The *Victory*, battle-scarred, being towed into Gibraltar after Trafalgar. By Clarkson Stanfield. *National Maritime Museum, Greenwich (Greenwich Hospital Collection).*

opposite, top right
Nelson at Vienna, 1800, by Friedrich Heinrich Füger, recently presented to the Royal Naval Museum, Portsmouth, by an American admirer of the admiral.

opposite, bottom
Gun-deck of HMS *Victory*.

below
Admiral Samuel Cornish, who in 1762 took Manila
for the British, with his secretary, Thomas Parry,
and his flag-captain Richard Kempenfelt (1718–1782),
in the cabin of the *Norfolk*, a typical mid-eighteenth-
century ship of the line. By Tilly Kettle.
Collection of T J Fenton, Esq.

of not being able to delegate. But in sheer energy and capability he was almost Nelson's equal, although he was ten years older. Tossing about in the Atlantic in an operational ship, he wrote the Trafalgar despatches in a style which was the admiration of the country for clarity, modesty and generosity to those who had fought. He continued to manage the business of the fleet, down to the last detail, for nearly five years after the battle, without a break of any kind, hardly ever setting foot ashore.

Many centralisers have narrow minds and limited interests. Collingwood was different. He saw and supervised everything, large and small. He could judge the possibilities in a youngster almost at a glance, such was his knowledge of men, and although he had no staff, not even a Captain of the Fleet, the Government trusted him to look after the whole complex of Mediterranean affairs, diplomacy included. They knew how lucky they were, but they had no reason to expect such talents in a naval officer. Ministers leaned upon Collingwood heavily, and in the end they wore him out.

Collingwood died a martyr to duty, though not altogether an unwilling one, for responsibility came naturally to him and he was as fearless of it as Nelson had been. Perhaps the greatest service of his later life (since he never had what he would have considered the good fortune to meet the enemy again in battle) was in encouraging, both morally and by ensuring supplies and communications, that upsurge of Spanish and Portuguese nationalism which was felt after Napoleon had supplanted the old dynasty at Madrid with his own brother. 'The Spanish ulcer killed me', the Emperor once remarked. He could not have paid a greater compliment to the army of Wellington and to the ships which supported it, for it was their strength which at last liberated Iberia from the French yoke.

In 1810, the year that Collingwood died, the British fleet reached its maximum strength under sail. There were 625 ships in commission, over a hundred of them ships of the line. 142,098 seamen and marines were in pay. This was over 30,000 more men than were serving at the end of the American War of Independence. In addition there were 23,455 Sea Fencibles, a force raised against invasion, and about 20,000 privateersmen who were exempt from impressment. Even so, and although the main convoy routes were well guarded, a formidable yearly toll was taken of British merchant ships by French commerce raiders, supported, at times most effectively, by those of Denmark. And, as always there were infinitely greater losses from sickness, and from what were known as 'marine causes', the normal hazards of the sea, than from shot and shell.

If Trafalgar had ensured that never again, during the remainder of the Napoleonic War, would the main fleet of France pose a serious threat to British sea predominance, there was an adverse side to this result. It led to arrogance and complacency. It deepened that conservatism which was a besetting sin in British naval affairs. Furthermore, while exalting Nelson into a kind of maritime patron saint, the naval establishment entirely failed to understand the reasons for his phenomenal success.

Shocks were in store. In 1807 'Orders in Council' were promulgated, in reply to Napoleon's 'Berlin Decrees' which established a blockade of Britain. The 'Orders' forbade neutrals to trade with France, under threat of seizure of their ships. The chief sufferers were the Americans, whose merchant navy had grown and flourished while Europe was at war. This fact, added to the annoyance caused by British captains stopping and searching American vessels for deserters from the Royal Navy, of whom there were many, led to hostilities in 1812. An American invasion of Canada failed, but the Americans gained control, after stiff fighting on Lake Erie, of the Great Lakes system, while in the Atlantic their well-built, fast and efficient frigates scored a number of successes that were felt by Britain to be deeply humiliating. In 1813 Captain Broke, of the *Shannon*, defeated the American *Chesapeake* within a few minutes outside Boston, and did much to restore the spirits of his fellow captains. The result was due to assiduous attention to gunnery, which far too many officers had neglected.

While Spain and Portugal had revived under the shield of sea power, much was happening in the old Spanish colonies in South America, where the first stirrings of independence had begun. It was a movement which quickly gathered strength in the absence of stiff opposition. It gave the British the chance to trade where this had once been forbidden, an opportunity which was eagerly taken. Thanks to the fleet, British merchants were given a long lead over their rivals. As was to be the case in Greece, the newly formed independent governments often had reason to be grateful for the quality of the British officers who helped them to form, man and operate their own navies.

After the defeat and exile of Napoleon, complacency returned and deepened. A series of small wars, mainly colonial, and a larger one against Russia in the 1850s, kept the navy in employment but added little to its reputation. The bulk of the work fell to the smaller ships, which proved their worth in the suppression of the slave trade. This was a slow process, for many nations, although paying lip service to Abolition, did nothing whatever to help to put slaving down.

In 1827 the Duke of Clarence, afterwards to succeed to the throne as William IV, and to become known as the 'Sailor King', was given the post of Lord High Admiral, which had been in abeyance for over a century. This went to the Duke's head. Although as a midshipman he had been in action under Rodney, and had at one time been a friend of Nelson, his active service had ceased thirty years earlier. His eccentricities

right
A drawing by James
Gillray showing the ways
of the press-gang.
*National Maritime
Museum, Greenwich.*

below
The *Victory* (right)
nearing home in January
1806: one of many
tributes to the Navy by
J M W Turner.
*From the collection of
Mr and Mrs Paul Mellon.*

soon made him a nuisance and he had to be put back on the shelf, but not before he had discovered that his beloved fleet was fast becoming a spit-and-polish institution, with gunnery neglected. He did what he could to put matters right, but he was not long enough in office. By the time he had become king, in 1830, many other matters occupied him.

As the decades went by, officers got older and older. The experiences of their youth receded ever more distantly. Their own remoteness from current developments, such as the use of steam for marine propulsion, grew increasingly apparent.

By 1860 the official Navy List told an extraordinary story. The single Admiral of the Fleet, Sir John West, was 86 and had been on the flag list for over forty years. There were 21 full admirals, of whom the youngest was 72. Every one of them had reached the rank of post-captain before the end of the Napoleonic War, not far short of half a century earlier. Two of them had been well known to Nelson. One was Jane Austen's brother, Sir Francis Austen, who had been on the chase of Villeneuve to the West Indies. He was 87, and had been a captain since 1800. The other was Sir William Parker, who had made a name for himself as a frigate captain. His promotion to post rank dated from 1801. There were 78 vice-admirals and rear-admirals, and 348 captains. Very few of them could ever hope for a command.

Gallant old Provo Wallis, who had fought under Broke in the *Shannon* that memorable day in 1813, had been on the admirals' list for a mere nine years, and had just been appointed a Knight Commander of the Bath. He was then 69, and he would one day–in 1877–rise to West's exalted place by tottering upwards by virtue of seniority. He died in 1892 at the age of over 100. By that time, Nelson's fleet had at last been transformed. Sail had almost vanished, except for training. The mine and the torpedo had been steadily developed. So had the reciprocating engine and the heavy gun. Even the submarine was becoming a factor to be considered by the leading naval powers.

A jolt, a major conflict, or a serious threat would be needed to revitalise still more thoroughly the Service in which Nelson had gloried. The necessary stimulus came in due course, though there was a long wait.

Admiral Lord Collingwood (1758–1810), Nelson's friend and successor. He fought at the 'Glorious' First of June, St Vincent and Trafalgar. By Henry Howard.
National Portrait Gallery, London.

THE IMPERIAL JAPANESE FLEET

opposite page
Admiral Togo
(1847–1934),
commander-in-chief
of the victorious
Japanese fleet at
Tsushima, May 1905.

It would have been a cause for astonishment to any European in the early years of the nineteenth century had he been told by a prophet that the first large-scale sea battle of the twentieth century would occur in the Pacific. He would have been even more amazed to learn that the victors would be an oriental nation, the Japanese, belonging to an island empire about whose way of life little was then understood.

Among Europeans, only the Dutch had a long-established foothold in the country, and even their activities were strictly regulated, though their leading representatives acted as the main channel through which the Japanese authorities could obtain such knowledge of the west as they sought. In a closed and intricately patterned society, such knowledge was not greatly in demand. The Japanese were convinced that they were secure. Their traditional way of life appeared to have divine sanction, while on the mundane plane they faced no immediate challenge.

The nation was, indeed, both martial and seafaring, with a long history of skill at arms. However, the principal type of Japanese fighting vessel of the sixteenth century and later, with a temple-like superstructure, and superlative craftsmanship in wood, was as differing in appearance, and in much else except for motive power (oar and sail combined), from anything then current in the Mediterranean or the Atlantic as could be imagined.

Ironically, in view of later events, the awakening of Japan to the realities of the outside world was largely due to the appearance of a United States squadron under Commodore Perry in Japanese home waters in 1853. As the vessels were steam-powered, they were the subject of intense curiosity on the part of the islanders. Ultra-cautious at first, and highly suspicious of western ideas and intentions, it was not long before those in power in Japan realised two things. The first was that if their country was not to be an anachronistic and picturesque survival from the past, they must study western ideas and absorb those which might prove useful. There was also the evident fact that if they did not speedily enlarge their interests, they could be at a serious disadvantage in the scramble for concessions of various sorts from the crumbling empire of China, which had for some time been pursued by the leading nations.

Expansionist countries had long controlled much of the Far East. First there had been the Spaniards, in the Philippines and elsewhere; then the Portuguese in Macao, the Dutch in the Spice Islands, the British in India, Ceylon, Burma and Malaya, while the interests of the French in Indo-China and in the Pacific were well known. The United States and Canada were developing their western seaboards, and there was Russia, an oriental as well as an occidental country.

Japan would have need of a friend among this group of nations, who were not often in accord with one another. She also needed a fleet if she was to make her influence felt and her wants known in the future. Britain was then the leading naval power, and in 1902, just within the lifetime of the present Emperor of Japan, an Anglo-Japanese alliance was formed, notionally 'for the maintenance of the *status quo* in the Far East'.

By that time Britain had already built and equipped a fleet for Japan, and had taught her craftsmen how to set about construction for themselves. The country was fortunate in the period when the ships were ordered, for since the coming of steam a succession of extraordinary and ungainly vessels had been produced in which first one characteristic – speed, or armour, or concentration of guns – had been emphasised, and then another. At one stage, as the result of a battle which took place at Lissa in the Adriatic between Austrians and Italians, there was even partiality for the ram. This was an almost laughably antique mode of destruction and superfluous when guns became efficient at long range.

By 1905, when the Japanese flagship *Misaka* was ready, she looked what she was, a trim and well-equipped man-of-war, fit to take on anything that floated. If she is taken as the measure of progress through the centuries, then it can be seen to have been slow. In 1588, the year of the Spanish Armada, a galleon might hope to cover something like 150 nautical miles in twenty-four hours. The *Victory,* over 200 years later, and with

a much-improved sail plan, might have managed 240 nautical miles, and the *Warrior* of 1860, under power, could be certain to cover 336. Forty-five years later, the *Misaka* could achieve 432, though like all steam-driven ships she was dependent on the grimy and time-consuming procedure of coaling by hand. This unpopular necessity came round all too often when high speeds were maintained.

In ordnance, the advance was remarkable. Right up until the early nineteenth century the naval gun was not effective at much beyond a mile, and the carronade, a battle winner at close quarters, had a still shorter range. But 12-inch projectiles shot from the business-like barbettes of the *Misaka* could hit targets eight miles away with lethal consequences. Greater speed and improved manoeuvrability had required guns to match. Inventors and armament firms met most demands. The torpedo had produced the fast torpedo boat, to which the antidote was the larger and faster torpedo boat destroyer. Ultimately, 'destroyer' was used as a generic term for maids of all work, ancillary to the line of battle. The other principal type of ship was the cruiser, very valuable on the convoy routes and for other duties.

It was not long after her fleet had been created that the opportunity came to Japan to prove its value. In 1895 there occurred an interval in the campaigning in China, for long an almost permanent occupation for Japan's well-trained soldiery. Japan was in possession of much Chinese mainland territory, including the Liao-Tung Peninsula with its dockyard at Port Arthur. She intended to keep what she held, but when the terms of the peace treaty became known, there was protest.

Russia, the northern neighbour of China along the borders of Manchuria and Mongolia, objected to the cession of Port Arthur to the Japanese. She argued that its permanent occupation by a foreign power would be a standing threat to the government at Peking, which was true, such was its geographical position. She induced France and Germany to join with her in demanding reconsideration of the terms. All three countries sent naval squadrons to the Far East, or reinforced those which were already there. Under threat, Japan revised the terms of the treaty and restored Port Arthur to China.

The concession meant that the nation had 'lost face', which to any oriental is a highly serious matter. Worse was to follow. The ink was scarcely dry on the treaty before Russia herself sought and obtained the right to build a railway through Manchuria to the port of Niu-Chwang, and, further, the right to garrison Port Arthur and to use it as a naval base. Although statesmen were dismayed by such barefaced cynicism, instead of doing something about it they watched in silence the continued provocation of Japan.

By February 1904 Japan was ready to act. She realised she must do this soon, for with the Ameri-

cans installed in the Philippines as the result of war with Spain, and European powers still more evident in China as the result of combined intervention in 1900 to suppress the Boxer Rebellion, her people were demanding that she make full use of the fleet which had cost so much of her revenue.

A torpedo attack was made on the Russians at Port Arthur on the night of 8 February. There had been no formal declaration of war and the Russians, taken utterly by surprise, suffered much damage, though no ships were actually sunk. They took time to recover. Even the use of minefields, in which they had long been adept, proved a doubtful advantage, for when on 12 April Admiral Makharoff, who was reported to be the best officer in the Service, offered battle to Togo, the Japanese Commander-in-Chief, the Russian flagship, the *Petropavlosk,* hit a mine and Makharoff was killed together with 632 officers and men. Even worse blows followed. The Japanese pursued their advantage by occupying the heights which surrounded the Russian base, from which they could bombard ships at anchor.

During August Admiral Witjeft took such ships as were available to him to sea, intending to join up with the Russian squadron at Vladivostock, but he was defeated and killed. The Eastern Squadron was no longer effective, and if Russia was not to be forced to accept a humiliating peace, the Tsar would have to send his Baltic ships round half the world in a bid to restore the balance. The difficulties were daunting, and the prospects at the far end were anything but encouraging. But with a grim sense of fatalism the squadron assembled, and in time proceeded on its way.

Admiral Rojdestvensky, the victim selected to conduct this odyssey, was badly served by intelligence and had no experience of ocean war. The original plan was that he should sail in July. His command was to include five 12-inch-gun battleships which were being completed at Kronstadt. They would work up to a state of battleworthiness during the course of their cruise. But completion of the ships was delayed, and even by October, when four were ready, the fifth had to be left behind, since weeks if not months more work were needed on her. Most of the Russian fleet was home built, but one ship, the *Tsarevitch* of 1901, had been designed in France, to which country Russia looked for ideas in construction just as Japan looked to Britain.

Forty-five ships started out, including a fleet train with essential supplies. A small group, led by Admiral Felkersham, would go by way of the Suez Canal. The rest would be routed round the Cape of Good Hope, and a rendezvous was appointed at Madagascar. The main body had a distance of 18,000 miles to traverse, and there was not a single Russian base on the way. However, France was helpful, and the Germans allowed the Russians to charter seventy merchantmen to keep the squadron supplied with coal.

below
Damage to the Russian
battleship *Tsarevitch*:
an impression by the
British artist Norman
Wilkinson, who depicted
three wars at sea,
including the two World
Wars.

opposite, top
A fanciful representation
of a Council of War,
1894, when the Japanese
Fleet was being built up.

opposite, bottom
The battleship *Fuji* of
1897, which took part in
the war with Russia and
survived as a training
ship until 1948.

The first incident reported by the world's press
was fantastic. One of the supply ships, which
had fallen behind with engine trouble, signalled
in the darkness of the North Sea that she was
being attacked by Japanese torpedo boats! Ships
began to fire at random, some against each other,
and a Hull trawler, fishing off the Dogger Bank,
was sunk with all hands. The British ordered a
cruiser squadron to shadow the Russians as far
as Gibraltar.

It was January 1905 before Rojdestvensky and
Felkersham met and took stock. The Russian
government had meanwhile decided to send a
further squadron of aged ships as reinforcements.
The whole fleet assembled off Indo-China on
15 May, ready for the run to Vladivostock. At no
time did it occur to Rojdestvensky that he might
beat the Japanese. It would be marvel enough if
he reached his goal more or less intact. News had
come of the fall of Port Arthur, and the expedition seemed increasingly unattractive to most of
those who took part in it.

On the night of 26 May a Japanese auxiliary
cruiser almost ran down a Russian hospital ship
in thick mist between the Korean mainland and
the Japanese island of Honshu. An hour and a
half later Togo was at sea, and by 7 a.m. on 27
May he had reports that the Russians were on a
north-easterly course, twenty-five miles north-
west of the island of Uku-Shima. They were
shadowed, but for some hours no fire was
exchanged.

By midday on the 27th, the anniversary of the
Tsar's coronation, Rojdestvensky was nearing
the southern end of the island of Tsushima,
with the signal: 'Steer North 23 degrees East for
Vladivostok' flying from the *Suvaroff*. Japanese
cruisers and destroyers were then seen in
strength on the port bow. Rojdestvensky ordered
his ships to form line abreast, a manoeuvre
which, though badly executed, caused the
Japanese to turn away. But at 1.20 p.m. when
Rojdestvensky had just re-formed into two lines
ahead, Togo was seen in the distance. His ships
were disposed so as to 'cross the T', that is to say,
he was on a course where he could bring all his
guns to bear against the advancing enemy, while
for their part, only the Russian forward guns
were of any use. It was a tactical situation which
Nelson had actually invited at Trafalgar in

海
軍
将
校
等
征
清
の
戦
略
成
論
す
る
図

below
An imaginative
representation of the
sinking of the Russian
ship Borodino at
Tsushima.

opposite, top
The Russian ships
Admiral Aprazin and
Admiral Seniavin,
captured in 1905 by the
Japanese and brought to
Sasebo.

opposite, bottom
Admiral Togo conducting
operations at Tsushima
from his flagship
Mikasa, which is still
preserved at Yokosuka.

order to produce a *mêlée,* but here the circumstances were totally different. Togo had brought about an opportunity such as was the aim of all admirals of the era of steam and the long-range gun.

The Russians were the first to open fire. Togo waited. When Rojdestvensky had approached to within about 6,000 yards, Togo began to concentrate his fire on the flagships of the two Russian divisions. One of them was soon set ablaze and began to sink. She disappeared soon after 3 o'clock. Rojdestvensky held on, but his ship was soon so badly damaged that she was forced to leave the line, since she would no longer answer her helm. The *Alexander III* took her place.

Rojdestvensky, who had been four times wounded and was unconscious, was removed to another ship, which was captured later. The *Suvaroff* herself remained afloat until the evening, when she was torpedoed and sunk. Soon the *Alexander III* went the same way, and so did the *Borodino,* whose magazines were pierced by a plunging shell which blew her up. With the onset of darkness, Togo left any further work of destruction to his destroyers, who made a night of it. They met very little opposition, the Russians being quite demoralised. By the morning of 28 May Togo still barred the way to Vladivostok, his battleships were intact, and Admiral Nebogatoff, who had become senior Russian officer, hoisted a signal of surrender.

As in so many naval battles, the losses were disproportionate. Six out of eight Russian battleships had been sunk, and two had been captured.

Fourteen other ships out of a total of thirty-seven which had been in action had either sunk or had run aground. Six had been captured. A further six managed to reach a neutral port, where they were interned. Only three, a light cruiser and two destroyers, reached Vladivostok to report the story of disaster.

Japanese losses were light. Three cruisers had been badly damaged; three destroyers had been sunk, and six or seven others needed repair. They had lost fewer than 600 men, as against ten times that number of their opponents. They thought highly of their ships and of their admiral who, as he went into action, flew a signal reminiscent of Trafalgar: 'The rise or fall of the Empire depends on today's battle. Let every man do his utmost'. They also noted the behaviour of a senior British officer who had been attached to them as an observer. In the middle of the fighting, he was seen to go below, at which there was some surprise, for he was renowned for his coolness. The reason was soon clear. His uniform had become the worse for battle, so he quickly changed it, returning to the deck immaculate.

The effect of Tsushima was to raise Japanese morale higher than ever before. Conversely, the Russians felt repercussions in places far from the Pacific. Ships mutinied in the Black Sea port of Odessa, the officers of the *Potemkin* being killed by their men, who then seized the ship and hoisted the red flag. The Russian government accepted an American offer of mediation, and peace was made. Japan obtained Port Arthur, this time without demur, and also the southern

half of Sakhalin, the long, narrow island off the coast of Siberia.

Japan had established herself as a naval power, and had proved herself against a European fleet. Within four years of Tsushima, the British naval attaché at Tokyo reported as follows:

... the Japanese Navy is at present in a high state of efficiency, and is of such strength as to render the position of Japan quite unassailable in the Pacific. The Navy has many weak points, as all navies have; but it has that paragon of advantages over any adversary that might come to attack it – 'fighting near its base'. The discipline and loyalty of the officers and men remain perfect; they seem to have few ideas outside their work; it absorbs their thoughts by day and effects their dreams by night.

In sum, the Imperial Japanese Fleet was single-minded, fanatically devoted to the service of the Empire. It was to remain so throughout the decades to come.

The Japanese fleet took little part operationally in the First World War, but as the ally of Britain the Emperor declared war on the Central Powers, Germany and Austria-Hungary. The effect was that her naval forces predominated in the Pacific, from which a German squadron commanded by Admiral Graf Spee departed.

Japan profited from the war experiences of both her ally and her enemies, and was able to increase her strength undistracted. This caused anxiety both in Britain and in America, their statesmen foreseeing that a state of imbalance in the Pacific was likely to result. Although the

below
A Japanese destroyer of
the First World War.

bottom
The battleship *Ikoma*,
1910, British in
appearance and design.

Anglo-Japanese alliance had been renewed in 1911 for a ten year period, matters grew increasingly difficult as a result of the Washington Naval Conference of 1922. Britain accepted naval parity with the United States, and the alliance with Japan ended. Japan agreed, not with any enthusiasm, to a proportion of five American and five British ships to every three Japanese, the differential being justified by the wider naval commitments of the U.S.A. and Britain.

Between the two World Wars there was much fine talk about collective security. Had the League of Nations, established in 1920, been given strength by the presence of the United States, more might have been done to check aggressors. As matters stood, Japan was the first major country to defy the League by her invasion of Manchuria in 1931. The act caused almost universal protest, but no power of any consequence was in a position to do anything about it. Had the event not been so serious and significant, more interest would have been taken in the sheer ingenuity with which Japan, having completed her work of conquest, established a puppet government. The Emperor K'ang Te, who at the age of three had become the last Emperor of China, and had been exiled three years later, was made President-Administrator. He was enthroned with great ceremony in 1934. None of the principal nations, with the exception of Germany and Italy, recognised the separate identity of what was renamed Manchoukuo, and it was not long before Japan was once more occupied with a war on the Chinese mainland.

Germany and Italy were both taking the path of expansion themselves, and were glad to align themselves with a nation with much the same aspirations. The Japanese plan was to extend the new 'Emperor's' dominions under her own direction. An old pattern was recurring in a slightly altered form.

The Second World War began in Europe in 1939. It seemed in the earlier stages as if it might be confined to that continent, and to the enlargement of Germany and Russia through the division of Poland and the absorption of the Baltic States which had enjoyed a precarious independence for less than twenty years. But when France fell in 1940, and Germany notified her ally, Japan, that, so far as she was concerned, she had a free hand in Indo-China, it was apparent that the struggle might soon be far-ranging.

The United States, although giving aid to Britain in what had become her lone struggle with Germany and Italy, remained neutral. But when, in the summer of 1941, Hitler invaded Russia, it was a sign that the Japanese should act quickly if they were to make the most of the greatest opportunity they had yet been afforded. America was not ready for war, and was vulnerable in the Pacific.

They struck their first blow in December 1941 without a declaration of war, just as they had done at Port Arthur over thirty years earlier. They attacked the American fleet at its base at Pearl Harbor. Although, by virtue of hindsight, it may seem to have been the rashest act conceivable, it was a deliberate and nicely calcu-

The battleship *Katori* of 1906, which served in the First World War.

lated risk, and it succeeded. The United States battle fleet was decimated in an air attack, although by great good fortune the aircraft carriers were not at the time at Hawaii. The battleships made a pyre of awe-inspiring dimensions, though they were, in fact, semi-obsolete and were never to regain their ascendancy at sea. The war would be decided by closely coordinated air-sea power, and by ships and aircraft supporting military landings when and where necessary. The aircraft carrier was soon seen as the principal capital ship, a fact which had been recognised by Britain some time earlier.

Japan was well supplied with every type of military aircraft and ship of war, and in the opening phases of her campaign, following up her initial advantage, she showed that her officers and men were splendidly trained, not least in night fighting, in the course of which she scored many successes.

Among the surprises of the war, at least to the western democracies, who had been accustomed to conduct even their military affairs and strategy far more openly than the countries ruled by dictators or dominated by military councils, was the enormous strength which could be deployed by what became known as the Axis Powers, particularly Germany and Japan, and also by Russia, engaged in what she called a Patriotic War. Secrecy, and the habit of unquestioning obedience, gave them immense advantages, and the dedication shown by their forces made it seem as if nothing was beyond their capacity.

It was thought, erroneously as it proved, that the Japanese might have shortcomings as airmen. A British aviation mission sent to the East in 1921–3 may have helped to give rise to this notion. If so, it was wishful thinking. The first Japanese aircraft carrier, the *Hosho,* was launched in November 1921 and the first take-off and deck landings were made in February 1923. Other carriers followed: the *Kaga, Akagi* and a

The Japanese cruiser *Asigara*.

above
Japanese destroyers
of the First World War.
A French heavy cruiser
is in the background.

above
Admiral Chuichi
Nagumo, who in
December 1941 led the
Japanese assault on the
U.S. naval base at Pearl
Harbor, and later fought
at Midway in June 1942.

right
Admiral Isoroku
Yamamoto,
Commander-in-Chief
of the Japanese Fleet
in the Second World
War until his death in an
air attack in 1943. He is
seen before the War as a
guest of the British
cruiser *Suffolk*.

number more. But, as in many other countries, Japanese experts were not convinced that the bomb had rendered the battleship redundant, and they continued to build very large ships of this type. The largest of all, laid down in 1937, were the *Musashi* and the *Yamato*, of 64,000 tons. They were armed with nine 18·1-inch guns, the largest ever to have been mounted on a ship. They carried seven aircraft, which could be launched from catapults. Another, the *Shinano*, was belatedly converted into a carrier. All three ships had short lives, the shortest being that of the *Shinano*. She was sunk during her trials by an American submarine, whose captain was no doubt overjoyed at finding so large and vulnerable a target.

Such was the initial force of the Japanese explosion in 1941 and the year following, outwards towards Hawaii, the Philippines, Indo-China and elsewhere, and such was the extent of its success, that it led Japanese strategists to attempt too much too quickly. The dissemination of the idea of an Asiatic 'Co-Prosperity Sphere', which was intended to appeal to the nationalism rising in so many countries of the Far East, had a measure of influence wherever it was backed by sufficient force. At the outset, this seemed forthcoming almost everywhere. The Americans were on the defensive. The miscellaneous assembly of ships hopefully assembled for the protection of the Dutch East Indies and Malaya, which included a British battleship and a battle-cruiser but no carrier, was soon defeated. Singapore, the naval base about which there had been much argument between the wars, proved to be what a historian had prophesied – 'a sentry box without a sentry'. When it fell, there seemed little to stop the Japanese from thrusting where they wished. Hard pressed as she was in the Atlantic and the Mediterranean, Britain had too few ships and aircraft to do more than check this formidable enemy even in the Indian Ocean, which the convoys were using for the later stages of their long haul to the Middle East via the Cape of Good Hope.

The American air-sea victory off Midway, which was won in June 1942, marked an important stage in the Pacific war. It was a battle of carrier forces, the opposed surface ships never sighting one another. The Japanese were made to realise that a democracy in which free thought was taken for granted, and discipline accepted rather than imposed, could produce as dedicated a navy as their own. Moreover it was one which called upon resources far beyond Japanese aspirations, in spite of her enormous territorial gains.

The decline in Japanese fortunes came about more through strategic errors than through any shortcomings of the Imperial Navy, which fought magnificently throughout. The idea of attempting to hold a vast 'defensive perimeter' stretching from the Aleutian Islands in the north to the Andaman Group in the Indian Ocean was unrealistic. Equally serious was the squandering of

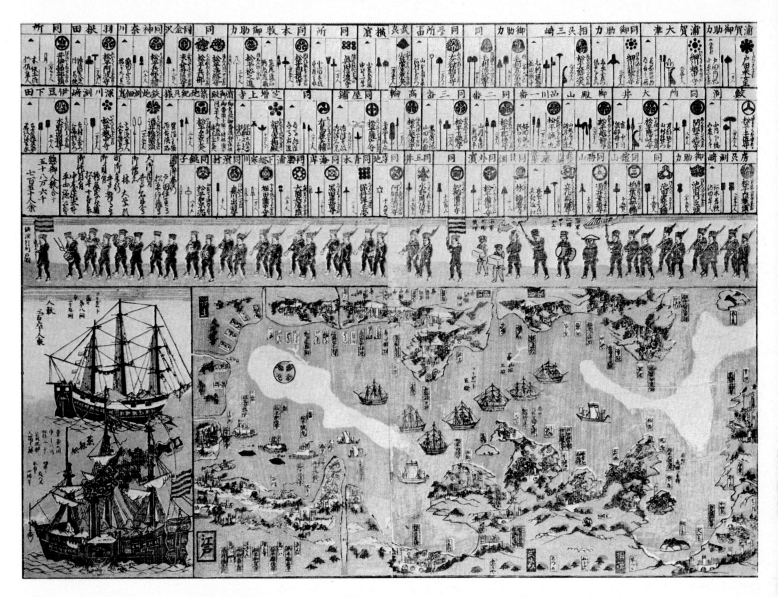

above
A Japanese print of the
United States visit,
1853.
*Franklin D Roosevelt
Library, Hyde Park,
New York.*

left
A naval engagement in
the Sea of Japan.
*National Museum of
Modern Art, Tokyo.*

below
The Japanese Fleet
bombards Port Arthur
during the Russo-
Japanese War.

right
The Battle of Tsushima,
28 May 1905.

帝國艦隊旅順攻撃

below
The Russian ship *Petropavlovsk* explodes a mine,
April 1904, and sinks with Admiral Makharoff.

opposite, top
The Japanese heavy cruiser *Mogami*, later hit and
sunk by U.S. air attack near the Surigao Strait in
October 1944.

opposite, bottom
The effect of air attacks on the Japanese cruiser
Mikuma at the Battle of Midway, June 1942.

merchant shipping. Not until more than a year after Midway did the Japanese adopt the escort-of-convoy system of protection, which the British had proved, by bitter experience in the Atlantic, to be the most effective way of countering the submarine. The change was made too late. By the end of 1943, Japan had lost nearly one third of her six million tons of shipping, and in the following year much of the rest fell to long-range submarines.

The main counter-offensive by the Americans began in the Solomon Islands in August 1942 and developed into a campaign of attrition. Japanese losses, particularly in aircraft, were heavy. So were American, but they were more than made good by the stream of new material pouring from the dockyards and factories. In November 1943 the Americans landed on Bougainville in the northern Solomons, and were able to gain naval and air bases from which the Japanese stronghold at Rabaul could be neutralised. The Gilbert Islands, far to the north-east, were seized three weeks later. Then a fast carrier force carried out a series of devastating attacks on enemy bases in the Marshall Islands, which had been Japanese Mandated Territory since the end of the First World War. This was a prelude to landings. In January 1944 Kwajalein, in the Marshalls, was

above
A Japanese naval bomber is shot down while attacking the U.S. Fleet off Okinawa during a later phase of the Second World War.

assaulted and held. A hole was thus punched through the vital Japanese perimeter.

In South-East Asia, the British sphere, the Supreme Commander, Lord Mountbatten, was starved of landing craft and other essentials for a large-scale offensive, owing to the exigencies of the war in Europe, and had to proceed more slowly. But the process of recovery continued steadily. The policy of island hopping was adopted by the Americans. Rabaul was bypassed. Manus, in the Admiralty Islands, which had a fine harbour, became a base for the elaborate fleet train which, in view of the immense distances involved in Pacific warfare, became of the first importance.

Gradually Allied forces approached the Japanese home islands, blasting their way by air-sea power, and by means of landings made against extremely stubborn opposition. The Imperial Fleet grew more and more attenuated, increasingly handicapped by shortage of fuel, so heavy had been the loss of tankers.

The Japanese produced no one, during the Second World War, with quite the aura of Togo, but their general standard of leadership was high. Their ships fulfilled expectations, except perhaps for the submarine arm, which on the whole had a disappointing war, partly due to

Vice Admiral Jisaboro Ozawa, who played a great part in battles with the U.S. Navy off the Solomon Islands, the Philippines and Leyte Gulf.

The Japanese hybrid ship *Ise* of 1943, combining a battleship's heavy gun-turrets with a stern flight-deck. Sunk in 1945.

above
The result of an attack by a Kamikaze or suicide pilot on the British aircraft carrier *Formidable* in 1945.

right
The battleship *Yamato*, 72,908 tons and armed with 18-inch guns, which was completed in 1940 as the largest capital ship afloat. She was sunk by the U.S. Fleet in April 1945.

opposite, top
Japanese single-seater naval aircraft operating from an island airfield during the Second World War.

equipment inferior to the Americans'. Until his death in an air attack in 1943 the Commander-in-Chief, Isoroku Yamamoto, retained the confidence of both his men and his government, and so to a lesser extent did Admiral Chuichi Nagumo, who had led the attack on Pearl Harbor.

During the final stages of the sea campaign the Japanese, in dire straits, took to a form of attack to which surface ships had long been vulnerable: assault by trained men prepared not merely to risk but to sacrifice their lives deliberately, with the near certainty that in so doing they would sink or cripple an enemy vessel. It was achieved by Kamikaze or 'Divine Wind' suicide pilots, who perished with the bombs they delivered.

Kamikaze was the name which had been given to a typhoon of the year 1281 which had destroyed two fleets sent by Kublai Khan against Japan. This time, no 'Divine Wind' could save the country, for Japan was beset on all sides. Even the Russians joined in against her at the last. Her proud fleet was in ruins, her merchantmen were sunk, her outlying military forces were on the verge of starvation. During the summer of 1945 atomic bombs were dropped on Nagasaki and Hiroshima. With their unearthly flash and all-consuming fury, an ultimate age in warfare began. Surrender was the only answer.

THE BRITISH GRAND FLEET

In the first Act of *Hamlet,* Marcellus, seated on the battlements of the castle at Elsinore, asks Horatio –

Why such impress of shipwrights, whose sore task
Does not divide the Sunday from the week;
What might be toward, that this sweaty haste
Doth make the night joint-labourer with the day;
Who is't that can inform me?

If Marcellus had addressed his question to any informed person in Britain during the earlier years of the present century, the answer would have been, Germany.

A new threat had grown to challenge the long supremacy of the Royal Navy. Marcellus' own country, Denmark, had been the first to feel it. That had been long before, during the troubles in Schleswig-Holstein, but one of the results had been the construction of the Kiel Canal and of an elaborate naval base at the neck of the Jutland Peninsula. The island of Heligoland, once Danish, then British, had been ceded to Germany in 1890 in exchange for rights in Zanzibar, and it had been fortified. Meanwhile, Germany was building such a fleet as had not been known before in northern Europe. No one questioned against whom it would be directed, for the sabre-rattling German Emperor had made this plain. The 'impress of shipwrights' on both sides of the North Sea was a recognised fact of life. If it were ever to slacken, it could only be after a major war.

The Grand Fleet which Britain assembled in the high summer of 1914, when the First World War broke out as the climax of a chain of reactions resulting from the murder of an Austrian Archduke at Sarajevo, was in purpose protective rather than destructive. Britain had a worldwide Empire to safeguard, and she possessed the largest mercantile marine afloat.

Of the battle fleets under consideration, those of Spain, Holland, France, Britain and the United States were all primarily protective. Sweden's fleet was different. It was originally designed for aggression, as was that of Japan, So, most of all, was that of Germany, a country which had no need of a fleet at all. That the aggressive fleets declined, while the protective type has endured may seem reassuring; yet their survival has at critical times been by narrow margins, and one cannot ignore the possibility that one day an aggressive fleet may provoke a universal holocaust, such are the means of war now available to those who can afford them.

Nelson's well-known prayer, written immediately before going into action at Trafalgar, included the sentence: 'May the great God whom I worship grant to my country *and for the benefit of Europe in general* a great and glorious victory . . .'. The italicised words are significant, for the admiral saw himself as the champion not only of Britain, but of what he regarded as civilisation. Few men have gone into action with quite such a wide conception at the back of their minds, but Nelson has not been unique in his vision. Certainly the creators of the Grand Fleet in 1914 felt themselves to be trustees for a fair and general use of sea power. Chief among them was Admiral Sir John Arbuthnot Fisher, later Lord Fisher of Kilverstone.

Fisher was an abrasive personality who removed the barnacles from an encrusted Service and brought it up to date. His patron saint was Nelson, though he was not at all like him. He called his sovereign, Edward VII, his 'Blessed Master' and was unusual in the reverence he accorded him. His obsession was the Fleet, which had long needed the attention of a man with ideas and the drive to carry them out.

It was Sir William Parker, a survivor from Nelson's era, who gave Fisher a start in the Navy, and the test he took before entry was characteristic of mid-Victorian times. 'I wrote out the Lord's Prayer', he recalled, 'and the doctor made me jump over a chair naked, and I was given a glass of sherry'. It was as simple as that, if you had a nomination from someone illustrious. Fisher lived until 1920, volcanic even in his old age, and as likely to erupt with a brilliant idea as a bad one. At close upon 80, just after the First World War had ended, he foretold the date of the Second, and he was right to within a year.

As was then usual, Fisher served in sail in his youth. He had no taste for it. One of his earlier ships, the *Calcutta*, took fourteen days from Portsmouth to Plymouth, owing to continual

right
Sir Winston Churchill,
First Lord of the
Admiralty 1911–1915,
with his successor, Lord
Balfour.

far right
Admiral of the Fleet
Lord Fisher (1841–1920),
creator of the British
Fleet of the First World
War. Bust by Jacob
Epstein.
*Imperial War Museum,
London.*

opposite, top
British ships visit Kiel
in the early summer of
1914. A Zeppelin airship
flies overhead.

opposite, bottom
HMS *Dreadnought*,
completed at
Portsmouth in one year,
which in 1906 made all
other battleships
obsolete. Nelson's
Victory is in the
background.

headwinds. Fisher was seasick, and summed up his feelings in a jingle:

Now sailors all take my advice
Let steamships be your motta
And never go to sea again
In the sailing ship Calcutta!

As he rose in rank, so his passion for modernity increased. He was a brilliant gunnery and torpedo instructor, with the habit of holding up his left hand when addressing his men, fingers and thumb extended, enclosing them in turn with his other hand as he made his points. The sailors called this act the 'four bananas and a baby's leg', and when told, Fisher roared with laughter. The Admiralty recognised his quality, and he held many of the key posts ashore and afloat until in 1904 he reached the head of his profession as First Sea Lord, where he remained for five years. His régime left foes foaming in his wake, as Winston Churchill put it, but he sponsored the *Dreadnought,* the first turbine-driven battleship. He encouraged the use of fuel oil because it led to efficiency, in spite of the existence of a widespread network of coaling depots. He wrote prophetically about the future of submarines, ships which, when first introduced into the Navy, were contemptuously referred to by the more conservative shellbacks as 'Fisher's toys'; and he saw the start of naval aviation. Churchill wrote of Fisher:

There is no doubt whatever that Fisher was right in nine tenths of what he fought for. His greatest reforms sustained the power of the Royal Navy at

the most critical period of its history. After a long period of serene and unchallenged complacency, the mutter of distant thunder could be heard. It was Fisher who hoisted the storm-signal and beat all hands to quarters. He forced every department of the Naval Service to review its position and question its own existence. He shook them and beat them and cajoled them out of slumber into intense activity. But the Navy was not a pleasant place while this was going on.

One of the most obvious reasons why it was not pleasant was because Fisher was a dictator. An officer was either in the 'fishpond', in which case he was looked after, or he was out on his ear. Then he was likely to make trouble, as did Lord Charles Beresford. There was more division within the Navy under Fisher than at any time since the American War of Independence, and he had no use for a Naval Staff. This was one of the matters where he was just plain wrong. Fisher wrote; during an embittered period in his life:

The savage instinct is still strong, and every human hates change – especially a change for the better. If you invent new cures for disease, they will burn you; if you are a patriot, they will shoot you; if you build up a business that employs a thousand men, you are a blighted capitalist, grinding the faces of the poor; if you compose divine music, you will die in a garret.

Fisher welcomed ideas from everywhere, if they served his ends. He was also a great one for anniversaries, if they could be made the occasion for something useful. Both these attributes were

right
In February 1915 an Anglo-French fleet bombarded forts at the entrance to the Dardanelles, giving the Turks notice of a full-scale attack to be mounted later.

below
A model of the cruiser *Glasgow*, launched in 1909, which took part in the battles of Coronel and the Falkland Islands, 1914, against the German squadron of von Spee. *Lent to the Science Museum, London, by the Fairfield Shipbuilding & Engineering Co. Ltd.*

to be illustrated in the case of the *Dreadnought*. The danger from torpedoes had made long-range gunnery necessary. Properly controlled fire meant salvoes from big guns each of the same calibre. In 1903 the Italian engineer Vittorio Cuniberti outlined his notions of 'An Ideal Battleship for the British Navy'. She would be of about 17,000 tons displacement, armed with twelve 12-inch guns, be protected by armour 12 inches thick over vital parts of her structure, and steam at 24 knots.

This was not a blueprint, but it was not far from a prophecy. In October 1905, the month of the centenary of Trafalgar, the first keel-plates of the *Dreadnought* were laid in Portsmouth Dockyard. The ship was launched in February 1906 and was ready for trials within a year – 17,900 tons of her. She was a first class ship, and she looked it. She had ten, not twelve big guns mounted in five turrets. Twenty seven smaller guns were fitted, to repel attacks from destroyers, and she was given five torpedo tubes. Her speed was 21 knots, far in excess of the battleships powered by reciprocating engines, and her main armour was only an inch less thick than Cuniberti had suggested. The *Dreadnought* rendered every other battleship obsolete, and, in spite of the speed with which she had been built, she fulfilled every expectation.

Two years later appeared the first of the battle-cruisers. They were splendid looking ships, though as a class they were ill-starred. The *Invincible,* the pioneer, was not very different from a battleship in appearance, and her displacement was very little less than that of the *Dreadnought*. But she had only 7-inch armour, and eight instead of ten 12-inch guns. Her great asset was exceptional speed. She could make $26\frac{1}{2}$ knots, and could outfight any cruiser then afloat. Others followed, notably the *Lion,* which was in service by 1912. She was huge for her day, nearly 30,000 tons displacement. She mounted eight 13·5-inch guns and had a speed of 28 knots. Her cost was £2,086,458, which for those times was an enormous sum, and she was followed by two other ships of similar design, the *Princess Royal* and the *Queen Mary*.

Battleships and battle-cruisers continued to leave the yards in a steady flow, each new type either an improvement on, or differing from the last. The most significant achievement in this race were the five *Queen Elizabeth* battleships. They were laid down in 1912/13 and completed during the war. They were the most successful capital ships designed by any navy, as their record was to prove. They were between 31,000 and 33,000 tons displacement, could steam at 25 knots, were faster than many battle-cruisers, had eight 15-inch guns and twelve 6-inch guns, and they were given an anti-aircraft armament.

The *Queen Elizabeth* began her operational career at the Dardanelles and ended it in the war against Japan thirty years later, having served at one time as the flagship of the Commander-in-

Chief, Grand Fleet. The *Warspite,* which like the *Dreadnought* was a product of the Portsmouth dockyard, had the longest roll of battle honours of any ship of her size, beginning with Jutland and ending with the invasion of Europe in 1944. Typically, when going to the breakers after the Second War, she broke away from her tugs and ran ashore at Prussia Cove on the Cornish coast. The *Barham* lasted until 1941, when she was sunk by a German U-boat in the Mediterranean, while the *Valiant* and *Malaya* survived both wars. It was an unparalleled record for a single class.

In July 1914, to be in readiness, the Grand Fleet sailed for distant Scapa Flow in the Orkneys. Such a base would have been inconceivable in any earlier war, when concentration was usually in the area of the Channel. This time, a new enemy called for new dispositions. At the outset Britain could call upon twenty-nine modern battleships and battle-cruisers, with twenty more in construction. German figures were twenty, with seven on the stocks. But such figures were misleading. British ships could never be available at maximum strength at any one time. There would be ships detached, ships repairing and ships refitting, since they were so much at

sea. It was otherwise with the Germans, in well-defended bases, able to exercise in the Baltic, and to conserve energy. It was chiefly in this respect that the maritime scene resembled that known to Cornwallis and Nelson, when the French sheltered in Brest and Toulon, while the British tossed about in all weathers.

The course of the war brought shocks, disappointments and dangers which had not been foreseen. Owing to Admiralty signals which led to uncertainty and confusion, a German battle-cruiser and cruiser were allowed to reach the Dardanelles and to proceed to Constantinople, where they became a principal means of bringing Turkey into the war on the side of the Central Powers.

The scene brightened at the end of August, the opening month of hostilities, when Admiral Beatty's intervention with the battle-cruiser force turned what looked like becoming an ugly situation in the Heligoland Bight into an outright British victory. But in the following month the U.9 torpedoed three cruisers in the North Sea in quick succession, and showed the value of the submarine against inexperienced captains.

Scarcely had the news been digested when a

Ships of the Battle-cruiser squadron led by Admiral Beatty (1871–1936). The *Lion* (flagship) is followed by the *Princess Royal, Indomitable* and *New Zealand.*

new battleship, the *Audacious*, was mined off Tory Island in the north-west approaches to the Irish Sea, and lost all power. The incident was alarming and significant for many reasons, although there was no loss of life. Investigation showed that the ship had hit a mine sown by the German armed merchant cruiser *Berlin*. The explosive charge did not exceed 160 lbs, whereas in both World Wars there were to be cases of far smaller ships surviving far larger explosions.

The Admiralty tried to keep the news secret, for in spite of efforts by the White Star liner *Olympic*, which was near at the time, the battleship sank after twelve hours of struggle to save or beach her. The particular wish for secrecy was due to the fact that, for the only time during the course of the war, the German High Seas fleet was equal in available capital ships to the Grand Fleet. It was no wonder that Admiral Jellicoe, who was in charge, and who, in a phrase of Churchill's, was 'the only man on either side who could lose the war in an afternoon' remained cautious. Any other attitude would have been irresponsible.

Another shock was the defeat of Admiral Cradock by Graf Spee off Coronel in Chile,

though he was swiftly revenged. Fisher had been recalled to the Admiralty and he sent off two battle-cruisers post-haste to deal with the German squadron, which was sunk early in December near the Falkland Islands after trying to break back to Europe.

In January 1915, what promised to be a sucessful battle-cruiser action near the Dogger Bank was broken off prematurely due to damage to Beatty's flagship, the *Lion,* to faulty signalling, and to mistaken concentration of British fire upon the sinking *Blücher,* the weakest ship in the German line. Correct tactics would have been to pursue and if possible annihilate a retreating enemy, but the chance was missed.

The Dardanelles campaign of the same year was a gallant failure, insufficient force being applied at the critical time in the hope of reaching Constantinople. A preliminary naval bombardment some months earlier had alerted the Turks, who had strengthened their defences. However, by far the greatest disappointment of all occurred off Jutland on 31 May 1916. In the only full-scale battle in the North Sea, the German High Seas fleet was allowed to escape, having inflicted far more damage than it had received.

below
A submarine at the Dardanelles in 1915, with a light cruiser and transports in the background.

bottom
Submarine B11 entered the Dardanelles, dived under five rows of mines, and torpedoed the Turkish battleship *Messudiyeh,* thereafter returning home safely.

right
The battle-cruiser
Indefatigable going into
action at Jutland on 31
May 1916. Shortly
afterwards she was
sunk by a heavy-gun
salvo which exploded her
magazine. The very light
armour of British
battle-cruisers made
them particularly
vulnerable to
long-range plunging fire.

below
Admiral Lord Beatty
(1871–1936) when
Commander-in-Chief,
Grand Fleet (centre),
with members of his staff.

Three British battle-cruisers were lost that day, as against one German battleship and one battle-cruiser.

The news of the clash was handled ineptly by the Admiralty, while the Germans, who got home first, made the most of it. It altered nothing. An American journalist remarked that the German fleet had assaulted its jailer but was still in jail, and a London versifier, with more sense of news value than those higher up, wrote:

The Germans cry aloud 'We've won!'
But surely 'tis a curious view
That those are conquerors who run
And those the vanquished who pursue.

The Germans had every right to be satisfied with the damage they had inflicted, but they remained blockaded, their merchant ships idle or interned. After some hesitation, they embarked on a campaign of unrestricted submarine warfare which at first was conspicuously successful. As the convoy system had not been introduced, British losses were soon so catastrophic that the whole war effort was threatened, and for a time Britain herself faced possible starvation.

The threat was mastered, convoys being belatedly organised, and the German strategy brought America into the war on the side of the Allies. There was one further highly sinister effect. Mutinies occurred in the German surface fleet, many of the better officers and men having been transferred to serve with the U-boats. For a time the mutinies were suppressed, but they recurred on a more serious scale in 1918. They were one of the many factors which led to the defeat of the Central Powers and to the surrender of their ships.

What Mahan called the 'silent pressure of sea power' had done its unspectacular work. Although soldiers sometimes complained of the Fleet's apparent inactivity while they were fighting in Flanders mud, every British battalion on foreign soil had been brought there by the Navy. The 'ultimate objects' set down by the Admiralty had been attained. They were as follows.

1. The protection of the Sea Communications of the Allied armies, more particularly in France, where the main offensive lies.
2. Prevention of enemy trade as a means of handicapping his military operations and exerting pressure on the mass of his people.
3. Protection of British and Allied trade on which depends the supply of munitions and food to the Allied armies and people.
4. Resistance to invasion and raids.

The four major components of sea power, the Fleet bases, the merchant navy and the shipbuilders, had all played their part. What had been lacking was a second Trafalgar, but this had not been necessary.

After the Treaty of Versailles had been signed in 1919 there was no need for the huge naval concentration that had been built up through the War, and in any case an impoverished Britain could not have afforded it. The axe was ruthlessly applied and many able men left the Fleet to find employment elsewhere. They had seen the Royal Navy at the apex of its might, and when they were recalled, as many of them were twenty years later, it was to face entirely different circumstances.

The Treaty of Versailles was followed in 1922 by a Naval Agreement at Washington as to the tonnage to be allowed for the immediate future. Battleships were not to be built exceeding 35,000 tons displacement and their guns were not to exceed 16 inches in calibre. They could be replaced by new ships only after at least twenty years in commission. Rebuilding was to be restricted to alterations for defence against submarines and aircraft. As a result, only two capital ships, the *Rodney* and the *Nelson*, were completed in Britain during the interval between the Wars. The *Hood,* which was within the battle-cruiser classification, was retained, having been commissioned too late to take part in hostilities. She displaced 41,200 tons, had a speed of 31 knots and was armed with eight 15-inch guns. She had cost, in 1920, £6,025,000, and she was in service for twenty-one years as the largest and best looking man-of-war afloat, as even foreigners admitted. When she was lost, in 1941, to a plunging salvo, going much the same way as the battle-cruisers at Jutland, it added one more tragedy to those which had already overtaken this type of ship.

When war broke out in September 1939, Winston Churchill was recalled to the Admiralty, from which he had departed in 1915 after disagreements with Fisher, chiefly about the Dardanelles. The plain fact was that there was no room for two dictators within the same department, particularly in time of war.

Word was signalled to ships and stations: 'Winston is back'. It may have heartened a few of the older officers, but could have meant little to younger ones, since Churchill had been out of office for ten years, and his well-informed warnings of danger had not been given much attention. Together with Marshal Mannerheim of Finland, he was to be the only man to hold preeminent posts in both World Wars. Both were recalled by reason of a national emergency, though long past their youth, both responded magnificently to the needs of the time.

Churchill found a navy tolerably well able to cope with the situation at sea so long as the alliance with France stood firm. There were fifteen battleships and battle-cruisers, and six aircraft carriers, although the *Courageous* was very soon sunk by a U-boat, another of which penetrated the defences of Scapa Flow and sank the battleship *Royal Oak* with heavy loss of life. The former title of Grand Fleet was no longer appropriate and it was not revived, but it was basically upon the Home Fleet, modest by older standards, and upon the Royal Air Force that the country was to depend during the next critical years, not only for prosecuting the war, but for survival.

The first important surface action of the struggle, indeed since that of Jutland in 1916, took place in the South Atlantic in December 1939 when a cruiser squadron under Commodore Henry Harwood intercepted one of the enemy's 'pocket battleships', the *Graf Spee*, off the estuary of the River Plate. The engagement was a classic of its kind, and had a moral effect far beyond South America. Harwood's force consisted of the 8-inch gun cruiser *Exeter* and the 6-inch gun cruisers *Ajax* and *Achilles*. The 11-inch salvoes of the *Graf Spee* damaged the *Exeter* so badly that she had to break off action and make her way to the Falklands for repair, but the smaller ships shadowed and harassed the battleship to such purpose that she put into Montevideo. Rather than accept action later with what her captain believed to be fresh forces, the ship was destroyed near the entrance to the port by her crew.

The prisoners the Germans had taken from the merchantmen they had sunk had been sent back to Europe in the supply ship *Altmark*. She was sighted in Norwegian waters in February 1940 and was boarded by a party from the destroyer *Cossack* under the orders of Captain Vian. The cry 'The Navy's here!' as British sailors entered the ship and released the men was a heartening one not only for those below, but for the nation in general, which had had little to cheer it in the first dark days of the struggle.

Any elation that was felt was short-lived, as a succession of reverses forced the Navy on to the defensive. First, Hitler occupied Norway and Denmark, and although the Navy continued to add to its laurels off Norway, it suffered heavy losses, including the aircraft carrier *Glorious*. The campaign in Holland and Belgium followed, and then the fall of France.

This meant that the Germans controlled the huge arc of coastline from northern Norway to Spain from which to wage war against an embattled and poorly-equipped island. The soldiers of the Expeditionary Force, which had been lifted by the Navy and an armada of small ships from the beaches of Dunkirk, had returned without heavy equipment, and there was little at

The first all-Dreadnought battle squadron in line ahead in 1910. Led by the *Dreadnought* (1906; 17,900 tons; ten 12-inch guns; twenty-seven 12-pounders; five torpedo tubes; 11-inch to 4-inch main armour belt; 21 knots) are the *Superb*, *Bellerophon* and *Temeraire* (all 1907), the *Collingwood* and *St Vincent* (both 1908) and the *Vanguard* (1909). Also shown are the last two pre-Dreadnought battleships, *Agamemnon* and *Lord Nelson*. By A B Cull, 1911.
Collection of Seymour Thistlethwayte, Esq.

FLOTTEN-
Schauspiele
Kurfürstendamm 153/156

opposite, top
The battleship *Thüringen* in action at Jutland.

opposite, bottom
The sinking of the *Scharnhorst*, December 1943, by
the British Home Fleet.
Collection of the Illustrated London News.

below
An early experiment in deck landing from the
carrier *Furious*, completed in 1916.

bottom
HMS *Eagle*, completed in 1917, and in service as a
carrier until sunk in the Mediterranean in 1942.

The Atlantic Fleet in 1925, led by the newly completed *Rodney*.

home to replace it. The entry of Italy into the war on the side of Germany added yet another to the problems, which in sum were greater than any which had confronted Britain since Napoleon arrayed his Grand Army on the opposite side of the Channel. For there now stood not only a new Grand Army, but an Air Force vastly preponderant in numbers.

Somehow, almost by a miracle of courage, improvisation, skill and defiance, the island held, and the daylight battle for dominance over the sky was won. To sustain the war effort was now the paramount necessity. Although President Roosevelt promised from America 'all aid short of war', the U-boats in the Atlantic and elsewhere began to take such a toll that there were stages when it seemed doubtful how long effective resistance could continue.

Badly as the war seemed to be going, there were signs that matters might improve. Admiral Cunningham in the Mediterranean had taken the measure of the Italians, and reduced their strength by sea, notably by a night raid on their fleet base at Taranto. Although his own force was reduced almost to ruins after the arrival of German air squadrons in the Middle East, his personal confidence was unshaken. When ship

opposite, top
The cruiser *Ajax*, Sir Henry Harwood's flagship at the Battle of the River Plate, 1939, with a notable record later in the Mediterranean.

opposite, bottom
A Swordfish aircraft of the Fleet Air Arm returning to the carrier *Ark Royal*.

left
Admiral Lord Cunningham (1883–1963), when Commander-in-Chief, Mediterranean, during the Second World War, on board the *Warspite*, his flagship, at Alexandria.

below
The final moments of the *Ark Royal*, sunk in December 1941 in the Mediterranean after strenuous war service.

after ship had been sunk or damaged in with-drawing troops from Greece and Crete, to which they had been sent to honour the pledge to aid all resistance to Germany and Italy, Cunningham was pressed by his staff to release the battered survivors from their task. 'No', he said, 'they must go on. It takes three years to build a ship. It would take three hundred to rebuild a tradition.' He found the necessary fortitude to endure crippling losses in the belief that it was vital that the Army should retain faith in the sister Service. His words were as memorable as those of Nelson at Trafalgar. They arose not only from the nature of the man, but because he had himself served alongside soldiers in South Africa, as well as having taken part in the amphibious warfare at the Dardanelles, where he had won the first of his many decorations for gallantry. At this stage of the war, such an example was of supreme importance, and in due time it would be won largely through the effectiveness of combined operations.

The two remaining capital ships belonging to the Mediterranean Fleet were severely damaged by daring attacks made from Italian submersible craft in Alexandria Harbour, yet somehow Malta was sustained in a long siege, and the strategic position in the Middle East was maintained, when according to most theorists it should have collapsed. And it was from the Middle East that the long struggle for Europe began, after America had been forced into the war by the Japanese attack on Pearl Harbor, and after Hitler had made his fatal decision earlier in 1941 to mount an attack on Russia.

The main antagonists were now arrayed in the

HMS *Chaser*, an aircraft carrier of 1942.

order in which they would continue and conclude the war: Britain and the United States, with Russia, against Germany, Japan and Italy. The Italians were to become a steadily diminishing factor, but from Germany and Japan the Royal Navy would suffer much. Already, a sortie by the new German battleship *Bismarck* and the cruiser *Prince Eugen,* in an attempt to disrupt the Atlantic lifeline, had occupied the whole of Britain's available naval resources before the *Bismarck* had been sunk. Even so, this had been at the cost of the *Hood.*

As for the Japanese, the war against them in the Pacific and the Indian Ocean opened disastrously everywhere. The battleship *Prince of Wales* and the battle-cruiser *Repulse*, lacking air protection, were sunk by bombs and torpedoes on 10 December 1941. This was a prelude to the

fall of the base at Singapore, and to an immediate threat to India. Before matters could be redressed, the ever-present threat from the U-boats had first to be contained, then mastered, and a number of operations set in train which would enable the Allies to gain a firm foothold in southern Europe, as well as to regain some of the positions from which they had been forced by the momentum of the initial Japanese advance.

By this stage, the British Fleet was manned by inexperienced sailors to an extent which had never been approached in any earlier conflict. This was particularly so with the smaller ships, the motor torpedo boats and gunboats which patrolled the Channel and the North Sea, and the landing and support craft which were vital to offensive operations wherever they were planned. A daring raid on St Nazaire by light forces

below
Escort carriers on operations in northern waters, 1943, with aircraft ranged on deck.

bottom
Two British light cruisers of the Dido class and one of the Edinburgh class steaming in line abreast in the Mediterranean during the Second World War.

in 1942 immobilised the biggest Atlantic dry dock available to the German navy, and in the autumn of that year, an Anglo-American armada appeared off North Africa as the essential preliminary to a series of invasions which began in Sicily and continued at Salerno during the summer of 1943.

The culmination of the naval war in the western hemisphere was Operation Overlord. This was the mighty amphibious attack on Hitler's Fortress Europe. It began on 6 June 1944 and involved almost every type of naval vessel belonging to the British and the United States Fleets. It was the most complex operation of its kind in history, including the creation of artificial harbours off the Normandy beaches for the unloading of essential supplies.

It was fitting that Admiral Sir Bertram Ramsay, who had had the melancholy task of supervising the withdrawal of the British Expeditionary Force from France in 1940, was in overall naval command four years later, with Sir Philip Vian, once of HMS *Cossack,* in tactical charge offshore of the British beaches. At the head of the Admiralty was Sir Andrew Cunningham, who in the previous year had succeeded Sir Dudley Pound as First Sea Lord. Pound had been a centraliser whose interference had led to disaster overtaking a convoy carrying essential supplies to Russia by the dreaded Arctic route. In contrast Cunningham believed in allowing his admirals to conduct their business with a minimum of interference from above.

The June assault succeeded, even beyond expectations, in spite of the uncertainty of the weather and characteristically stubborn resis-

Admiral Sir Bertram Ramsay, commanding Allied naval forces, at the invasion of Normandy, 1944.

tance. After the success of the D-Day landings it became possible to release substantial British naval forces to join those of the United States in the culminating stages of the war against Japan.

Much has been made of British reliance on American resources at all stages of the naval war, particularly in the Pacific. But there was in fact another side. There is a plaque in the Portsmouth dockyard, presented by Americans in appreciation of the fact that at the height of the struggle so many of their ships benefited from its resources.

The Second World War brought few surprises to the Home Fleet, which had been prepared for almost any contingency, with the exception of the loss of every Continental base. What was new was the intensity and the sheer scale on which the Second War was fought. For while the wars of the time of Napoleon, and even of Louis XIV's era, had affected much of the world, they had never spread to the Pacific, where fighting at sea dwarfed anything that had hitherto been known in maritime history.

It took nearly four years of intensive effort before the U-boats were mastered, largely by the application of air power, and there was always the possibility that serious crises would recur. The aircraft carriers building in Britain at the outbreak of war were outstandingly successful, not the least of their qualities being their armoured flight decks. These saved them more than once from destruction, both in the Mediterranean, where the *Illustrious* survived direct hits by heavy bombs, and in the Pacific, where they were exposed to the sacrificial efforts of the Japanese suicide pilots.

below
HMS *Warspite* shelling enemy positions, Normandy, 1944.

bottom
Convoy to North Russia by Charles Pears. *Imperial War Museum, London.*

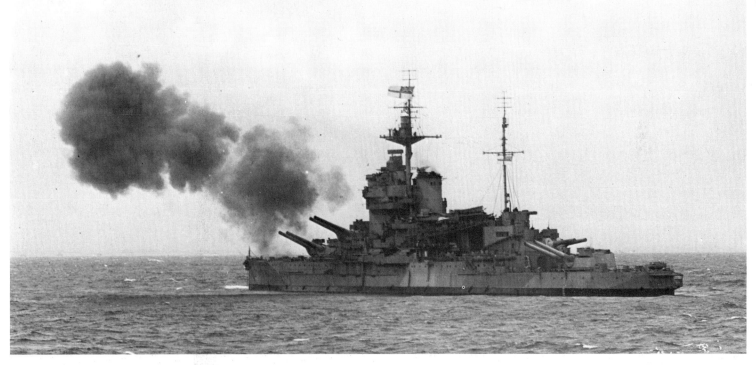

Although battleships became relegated to a secondary rôle, they continued to be of high value in task forces, for bombardment duties, and in the protection of convoys. The sole surviving battle-cruiser, the *Renown,* which had been laid down in 1916, served with distinction in many areas, and although she did not justify Fisher's original hopes for her class, her record was an exceptionally fine one.

As for the submarine arm, British submarines were used with great effect in both Wars. In the First, their penetration into the Baltic, and into the Sea of Marmora during the Dardanelles campaign, caused consternation and did great damage, though the vessels themselves lacked many of the technical advantages which the Germans later brought to perfection. In no department, least of all in the smaller ships, did the Grand Fleet or its successor fail. Although after the Second War the Royal Navy had to accept a far less important place in the maritime hierarchy than it had once enjoyed, the quality of its officers and men has been maintained.

The day of the aircraft carrier, like that of the battleship, now appears to be over, certainly in the form in which these ships were employed between 1939 and 1945. The rôle of the submarine has become increasingly important; with nuclear-powered machinery, and armed with ultra-sophisticated long-range missiles, its capabilities as a deterrent may be decisive.

Although the British Fleet now has a more modest part to play than at any time since the reign of Elizabeth I, it is still respected by the fleets of other nations. It remains true to its well-tried belief that nothing is impossible.

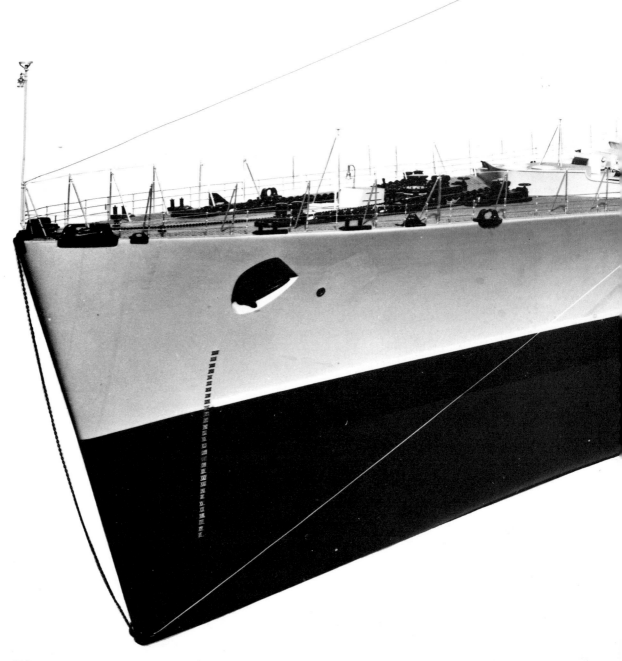

Model of HMS *Vanguard*, completed in 1944 as the last British battleship.
Lent to the Science Museum, London, by John Brown & Co. Ltd.

THE GERMAN HIGH SEAS FLEET

The political unification of Germany, at the head of which was an Emperor who was also King of Prussia, dated from 1871 and was the culmination of the work of Bismarck. But the German Empire had been preceded by two looser organisations which might have been made to serve the same end. The first was the Confederation of 1815, which included Austria. The second, a North German Confederation of 1866, was formed after Austria had been defeated by Prussia.

German aspirations towards the establishment of a fleet dated from at least as early as 1848. In that year a remarkable silver medal was struck. On it was seen the figure of Germany, crowned, with shield and spear, seated on a wharf with a trophy at her feet, with ships in the distance. A legend was inscribed: 'May the Navy carry the German eagle over distant seas and protect it. The German Fleet, a monument of national vigour and unity of Empire, founded by order of Parliament at Frankfort'.

There is much which is strange and prophetic about this medal. It appeared simultaneously with troubles in the duchy of Holstein, which was German-speaking. It spoke of Empire before such a conception had been realised, and it referred to a parliament at Frankfort, not the famous city on the Main, but the city east of Berlin. It was in fact in Prussia that the impetus towards the building of a navy began, and where it was to continue.

The year 1848 was one of revolutions and revolts in Europe, in which the Holsteiners joined so thoroughly that their country was plunged into war. The separatists, who wished to become Germans instead of subjects of the King of Denmark, were given active help by Prussia, and in April 1849 there occurred the earliest Baltic battle in which steamships were engaged.

This was at Eckernförde Fjord, off Kiel Bay, when the Danes attempted to use their navy to cover a landing against the Holsteiners. The *Christian VII,* 84 guns, and the smaller *Gefion* were sent into the fjord, together with two steamers. The shore batteries were well manned, and after a fight lasting most of a day, both sailing ships surrendered. The *Christian VII* was so

badly damaged that she had to be broken up, but the *Gefion* was taken into the Prussian navy and rechristened *Eckernförde* in honour of the victory. The Danes lost over a hundred killed and sixty wounded in proving what their ancestors could have told them from experience, namely that sailing ships have a poor chance against shore artillery in good positions.

More sinister was the appearance, shortly after this episode, of a German submersible craft, the *Brandtaucher,* the invention of Wilhelm Bauer. Her mere presence was enough to cause a Danish blockade of Kiel to be lifted. The *Brandtaucher* was operated by a three-man crew, one at the helm and two turning the propeller. She was one of a series of such experiments, which can be traced back at least as far as the American War of Independence, when David Bushnell tried and failed in a plan of attack on Howe's flagship in New York harbour, his submersible being operated by Sergeant Ezra Lee. After one successful trip the sides of the *Brandtaucher* collapsed, and her crew were lucky to escape with their lives. In 1935, sixty years after Bauer's death, when the Germans were starting to build up a submarine fleet which they hoped would surpass that of the First World War, they struck a medal in the inventor's honour.

The rebels were at last suppressed by the Danes, though not for long. In 1864 Prussian and Austrian forces invaded the duchies of Schleswig and Holstein, defeated the Danish army, and this time Prussia got her way. The territories were annexed, including Danish speaking areas. There was much protest, but no great Power was prepared to act.

The principal naval engagement was an inglorious affair. Baron von Tegetthof, sent from the Adriatic in charge of an Austrian squadron to help the Prussians, surprised three Danish ships of equivalent strength to his own, off Heligoland, on 9 May 1864. He attacked at once, but met with stiff resistance. Although three Prussian ships arrived on the scene, they were ineffective. The Danish commodore managed to retreat to the protection of shore batteries without loss. His own squadron scored ninety-three hits on Tegetthof's flagship, the armoured frigate

193

from left to right
Obverse and reverse of a medal of 1897 by H Durrich signalising a great expansion of the German Navy; obverse and reverse of a medal by K Lange marking the formation of a German Navy in 1848.
Both National Maritime Museum, Greenwich.

Schwarzenberg, and caused fires. Tegetthof subsequently did better at Lissa against an Italian fleet when, in 1866, Prussia turned on her ally. But he could not save Austria from defeat and humiliation at the hands of Prussia.

With Denmark, Austria and France beaten, and the Empire established, the German dream was realised. Nothing seemed beyond her, including expansion overseas. For that, she required a powerful fleet, the building of which would inevitably antagonise Britain and France. She joined in the scramble for territory in Africa, and in the exploitation of China. During the course of the Boxer troubles of 1900, the efficiency of the German naval contingent impressed other nations, as did the advent of their men-of-war in many parts of the world which they had not previously visited.

In creating a navy almost from scratch, the Germans had the great advantage of being able to make use of the results of that protracted experimentation in design which had long engaged constructors in Britain, France and Italy, without the expense of discovering drawbacks and defects for themselves. They had adequate raw material at hand, or quickly available, and immense technical skill. Admiral Fisher's opposite number in Germany was von Tirpitz, the Emperor's Minister of Marine. He was the inspiration of two Navy Laws, one dating from 1898 and the other from 1900. They authorised the transformation of the existing maritime defence force into a High Seas Fleet.

Matters were speeded by the personal attitude of Wilhelm II who, though himself an Emperor, envied the altogether serener majesty of his grandmother, Queen Victoria, and his uncle, Edward VII. Bursting with self confidence and full of high words, the Kaiser was capable of producing his own designs for cruisers, and of lecturing his admirals on how to conduct a naval engagement. He had been greatly impressed by Mahan's books on sea power, which began to appear at the end of the nineteenth century, at the very time when the German High Seas Fleet occupied so much attention, and was to engage so large a proportion of German resources.

Mahan, like Marx, Darwin and a handful of others, could fairly claim to have affected the course of history through the dissemination of ideas which became part of the mental equipment of thoughtful people. He was not always right, for instance in later life he disapproved of the all-big-gun battleship, since he preferred a mixed armament, but he was immensely persuasive and his exposition of principles for the exercise of sea power has not been seriously challenged. The Kaiser's mistake was in trying to draw lessons from Mahan which, while applicable to Britain or to the United States, did not apply to a country, such as his own, which was not *dependent* on a fleet for security and well-being. Germany already had the most formidable army in Europe; a fleet was a luxury.

Bismarck's aims, in the acquisition of Schleswig and Holstein, took in far wider matters than the 'liberation' of the German speakers. Among them was included the building of the Kiel Canal. In this respect Schleswig, the northern duchy, was useful in providing additional territory for defence in the unlikely event of an attack from Denmark. A strategic canal of this sort had been projected in the past and the full scheme was realised in 1895. Yet another series of medals was issued, celebrating the opening. This time the wording on the most imposing example ran: 'Through the flooded land, which once rang with German song, now proud masts are strung out upon the German waters, whether for war or peace'.

Prussia had by this time absorbed Hanover, so that those great outlets to the Baltic and to the North Sea, the mouths of the Ems, Weser, Elbe, Oder and Vistula, were in Prussian hands. The splendid harbour at Kiel had been particularly coveted by the far-sighted Bismarck, for a waterway had only to be driven between it and the mouth of the Elbe, and what nature had

given to Denmark could be taken from her. A new key to the Baltic had been forged by Prussia, which was now able to move her ships of war from the North Sea to Königsberg at all seasons of the year without political or maritime let or hindrance. It was a striking example of how sea power can unite as well as divide. The acquisition of Heligoland, which had been of value to Britain during the Napoleonic War as an entrepôt for trade, but which was too near the German coast to be easily defended in time of war, helped to strengthen the position which Bismarck had gained for Tirpitz. The nature and composition of the future German fleet remained to be decided.

Was it to be a true High Seas Fleet, with the capability of making prolonged voyages? If on the other hand its strength was to be concentrated in home waters, no provision need be made for an extended cruising range. More thought could be given to armour, less to fuel requirements and to the comforts of officers and men. In this respect Britain had no choice. Her fleet was expected to proceed anywhere and at any season.

A characteristic of Germany, and more especially of Prussia, has been the seriousness with which every aspect of war has always been studied. Prussia was transformed from a comparatively unimportant state into a mighty one through the capacity of her military leaders, particularly Frederick the Great. Her army was her pride. If her fleet was to take its rightful place beside it, no effort must be spared to make it the best of its kind. If she arrived belatedly on the maritime scene, Germany must show strength and even splendour. She had admirable dockyards and shipbuilders, and her transatlantic liner *Kaiser Wilhelm der Grosse* won the blue riband for the fastest east-bound crossing in 1897, a record which was retained by German ships for a decade.

Tirpitz's original programme foreshadowed the building of nineteen battleships, eight armoured defence ships, six large and sixteen smaller cruisers, and appropriate destroyer flotillas, within a period of seven years from the passing of the Navy Law of 1898. The *Kaiser Barbarossa,* launched in 1900, was typical of a series. She was closer to contemporary French ships than to British, and she displaced 11,150 tons. She had a mixed gun armament and five torpedo tubes. Her three propellers gave her a speed of 13 knots. She looked workmanlike and proved to be so.

When in due course it fell to the German designers to reply to the *Dreadnought,* the result was predictable. Their ships were shorter and beamier than the British; their displacement was slightly more; they were given ten 11-inch guns, and their speed was 20 knots. The use of triple screws was favoured by the German engineers, as it was by the French navy.

Tirpitz followed Fisher's lead in building battle-cruisers. The *Derfflinger,* completed in 1914, was perhaps the most representative of her type. She had thicker armour than contemporary British examples. She mounted eight 12-inch guns in the centre line of the ship, and she was designed for a speed of $16\frac{1}{2}$ knots, which was much the same as that of her predecessors, the *Moltke, Goeben* and *Seydlitz.*

When war began in 1914, the principal German ships outside home waters were those of the China Squadron under Graf Spee, including the crack cruisers *Scharnhorst* and *Gneisenau* and some light cruisers, one of which, the *Emden,* enjoyed a run of success before she was sunk by the Australian cruiser *Sydney,* and the *Goeben* and *Breslau* in the Mediterranean. They proved that Britain would have much to occupy her, so well were they handled. Besides their submarines, which were soon to show their abilities, the Germans also possessed, in their huge Zeppelin airships, a means of sea reconnaissance of which much was hoped.

The submarines remained a threat throughout the war, and in time they became the chief one. The Zeppelins, due to the often unfavourable

from left to right
Obverse and reverse of a medal by K Gotz honouring Wilhelm Bauer (1822–1875), whose primitive submersible craft, used against Denmark in 1850–51, foreshadowed U-boat campaigns of the two World Wars; obverse and reverse of a medal of 1895 celebrating the opening of the Kiel Canal; a medal to honour Grand Admiral von Tirpitz (1849–1930). *All National Maritime Museum, Greenwich.*

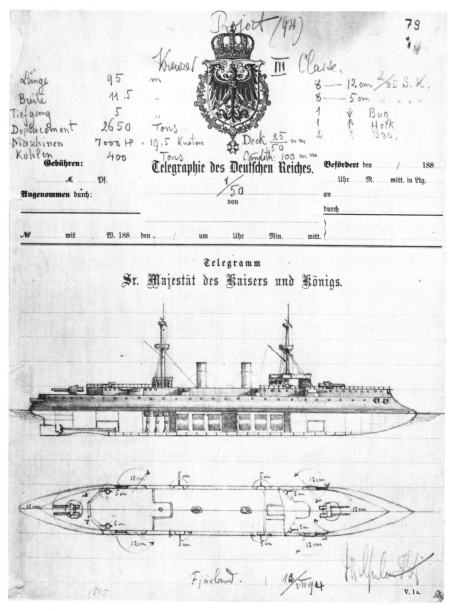

above
A design for a cruiser, made on a telegraph form by Kaiser Wilhelm II (1859–1941). *Bundesarchiv, Berlin.*

right
From left to right: Kaiser Wilhelm II (1859–1941), Grand Admiral von Tirpitz (1849–1930) and Grand Admiral von Holtzendorff (1853–1919) on board the Imperial yacht *Hohenzollern* in 1910.

opposite page
Battleships of the High Seas Fleet exercising, watched by Kaiser Wilhelm II (holding the rail in the foreground).

weather conditions over the North Sea, did not take a leading part in the naval war, but were employed in raids on England. Those who are old enough to remember them at first hand are not likely to underrate their effect. In the early war years, British naval aviation was much employed on their account.

During the course of the battle-cruiser action off the Dogger Bank in January 1915, the Germans learned lessons they put to good use. One of their ships, the *Seydlitz,* was badly hit by a British salvo, and was only saved from blowing up by flooding the magazines. They realised from this incident the dangers arising from flash, and although their arrangements for handling ammunition were already safer than those of the British, they improved them further. They also learnt something about the fighting capacities of Admiral Beatty, which was useful to them during the earlier phases of the battle of Jutland.

This extended action, during the following year, was the only full-scale fleet encounter of the entire war. Scheer, the German Commander-in-Chief, had hoped to trap the British battle-cruiser force before the Grand Fleet could come to its help, and to destroy it. The plan failed, and both sides became the victims of surprise. Beatty, when his battle-cruisers engaged those of Hipper, was soon faced with heavy loss due to magazine explosions which destroyed the *Queen Mary* and the *Indefatigable.* The *Lion* was only saved from going the same way by an officer of Marines, who ordered a magazine to be flooded, although himself mortally wounded. Thanks to his earlier experiences Hipper had no such crises, but his ships suffered terrible damage, much of it from the fire of four *Queen Elizabeth* class battleships which had been attached to Beatty.

Scheer was unaware that Jellicoe was even at sea with the Grand Fleet. He was lured towards Jellicoe by Beatty's skill and tenacity. When the fleets met, Scheer found that Jellicoe had so deployed his battleships that the Germans faced an arc of fire stretching to the horizon. The British admiral had 'crossed the T', just as Togo had done at Tsushima. Scheer saved himself, not once but twice that day, by an exceptionally difficult manoeuvre. The Germans called this the *gefechtskehrtwendung* or 'battle turn-about', every ship simultaneously reversing course at high speed. It had never been carried out under fire, and it was done so well on 31 May 1916 that it was a mystery for some time to British tacticians as to how Scheer had escaped almost certain destruction.

The High Seas Fleet was better at signalling, and in night fighting arrangements, than the Grand Fleet, and the way in which Scheer got his ships back to their base during the brief hours of summer darkness reflected the greatest credit on his skill and on that of the subordinate admirals and captains. The actual losses in the battle were: *British:* three battle-cruisers; three cruisers; and eight destroyers. *German:* one

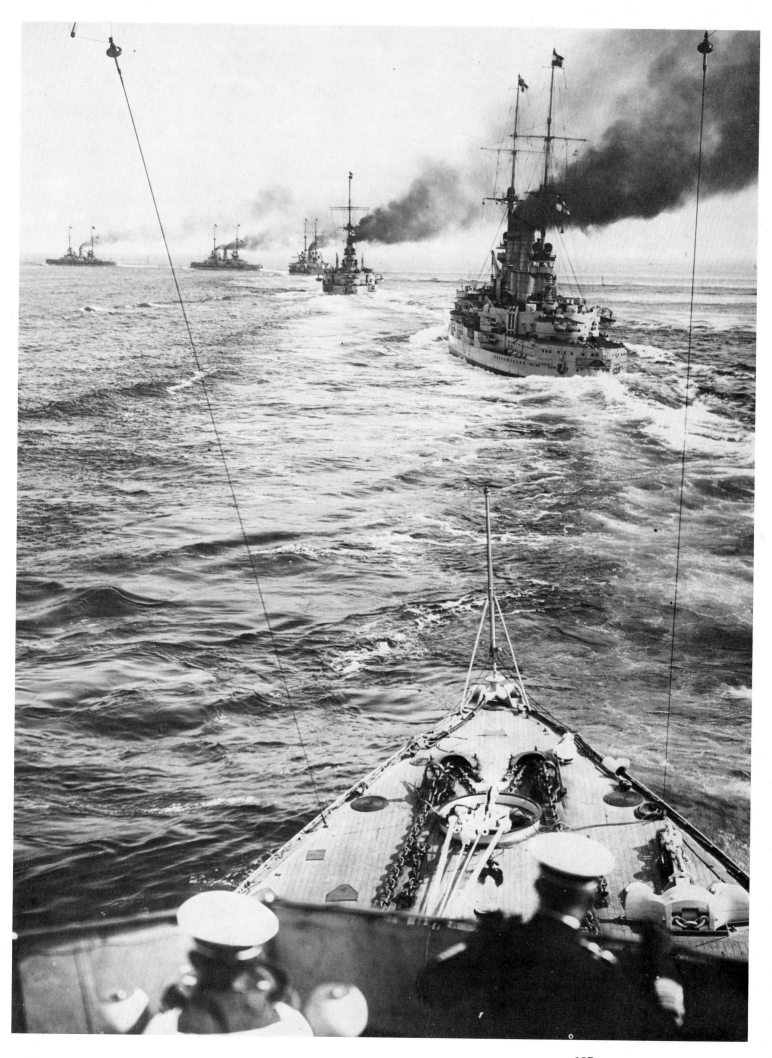

below
The High Seas Fleet of 1914, a battleship of the *Thüringen* class leading the line. The group on board the ship on the right includes (centre) Grand Admiral von Tirpitz.

opposite, top
The cruiser *Breslau*, which accompanied the *Goeben* to the Dardanelles in 1914.

opposite, bottom
The battle-cruiser *Goeben* which, with the cruiser *Breslau*, entered the Dardanelles in August 1914 and helped to bring Turkey into the war alongside Germany.

battleship; one battle-cruiser; four cruisers; and five destroyers. In the Grand Fleet 6,097 officers and men were killed: in the High Seas Fleet, 2,551. The numbers of wounded were about the same: British, 510; German, 507.

Because it presents so many points of interest to students of strategy and tactics, Jutland was studied and refought for years afterwards in war colleges all over the world. A witty American officer, bemused by the complexities, was once heard to murmur that he thought it was 'a major defeat for the U.S. Navy'. In all, there had been 250 ships present, 151 British, 99 German. There was a solitary reconnaissance made by a British seaplane from the carrier *Engadine,* while a Zeppelin flew high over the battle area, unaware of what was going on below! Not until Leyte Gulf, which was fought between United States and Japanese forces in October 1944, were more ships involved in an action at sea.

Very early on in the war, the Germans had been relieved to realise that, whatever happened by land, they would not have to wage a serious sea war on two fronts, for the Russian navy proved not to have recovered from the setbacks in the Far East which they had met with in fighting Japan. After the Revolution of 1917, the Russians could be disregarded altogether in the Baltic. However, they did render one important service to their allies. In 1914 the German cruiser *Magdeburg* was destroyed in the Gulf of Finland. Some of the ship's confidential books were found by divers, and the signal codes were sent to London.

The German surface navy produced a splendid leader in Hipper, and both in men and material, particularly in the stoutness of the ships, it proved to be outstanding. Even so, its efforts paled beside those of the U-boats. The submarine arm had been developed later in the German navy than in the British, but extraordinary attention was given to it from the outset. Many of the best of the younger officers found an outlet for their initiative and resource not only in attacks on Allied ships of war, but in the merciless warfare against merchantmen which covered the floor of the sea with wreckage. An exceptional U-boat commander could be sure of destroying a vast amount of tonnage, all of it vital to the war effort.

Very early on, U-boats were operating as far from their home waters as the Mediterranean and the Aegean, for they had the use of Austrian bases. The earlier British submariners also had remarkable records, but their opportunities were much more limited, for there were few

right
Admiral von Spee
(1861–1914), victor at
Coronel, 1914, and
defeated the same year
off the Falklands.

below
Damage to the cruiser
Frauenlob after action in
the Heligoland Bight,
August 1914.

German merchantmen to sink. Once submarine warfare was decided upon as Germany's main sea offensive, vessels poured from the yards, an astonishing effort in view of the strain which a land campaign on two fronts inevitably entailed. Not the least remarkable among German feats were two transatlantic trading voyages made by the submarine *Deutschland* of 1,500 tons. These were achieved in 1916, the year of Jutland, and they had some propaganda effect in the United States, as demonstrating a new way in which the Allied blockade could be evaded. Submarines were also extensively used for mine-laying, a rôle which, before the war, had been considered as likely to be more effective even than torpedo attack, such were the shortcomings of the earlier types of torpedo. The war improved every type of weapon and these improvements were permanent.

After over four years of warfare of an unprecedented ferocity, the Germans agreed to the terms of an Armistice. Wilhelm II shamed his office by steaming in a treasure-filled train to the sanctuary of neutral Holland, while his people endured the humiliations of defeat and of near-starvation due to the effects of blockade.

On 20 November 1918 submarines began to report to Harwich, there to await scrapping. Next day the British Grand Fleet sailed for the last time, in company with American capital ships, to meet and escort eleven dreadnought battleships, five battle-cruisers, ten light cruisers and fifty destroyers to Rosyth. Most of these ships proceeded later to Scapa Flow and there, during the following year, they were scuttled by secret arrangement. Their crews had long been demoralised, and the officers were virtually prisoners of their own men. The proud days of the German High Seas Fleet soon became a memory, though it was to prove to be an evocative one.

By the terms of the treaty of Versailles, Germany was allowed to retain six battleships, which were not to be replaced by vessels larger than 10,000 tons. Submarines were forbidden her altogether. These clauses were evaded or defied, for the Germans nursed the intention of avenging a defeat which they blamed on 'betrayal'. Within ten years, her naval constructors had designed, in the 'pocket battleship', a vessel which, though within the stipulations of the Treaty, was swift enough to run from most capital ships, with her speed of 26 knots, while her armament of six 11-inch guns was strong enough to defeat any cruiser. The *Deutschland*, pioneer of her class, was laid down in 1929. She was so successful that she was followed by two sister ships, the *Admiral Scheer* and the *Admiral Graf Spee*. The Germans were eager to commemorate their leaders of the First World War.

By the time the pocket battleships were fully in commission, Hitler had come to power in Germany and rearmament was going ahead openly on a massive scale. The nation was apparently eager to resume the waging of war, at which it was so expert. In 1934 construction was begun on the 31,300 ton battleships *Scharnhorst* and *Gneisenau,* armed with nine 11-inch guns and with a speed of 32 knots. By September 1939 two much larger ships were in hand, the *Bismarck* and the *Tirpitz.* Their displacement was 52,600 tons: they mounted eight 15-inch guns and had a speed of over 30 knots.

As so often in history, defeat was of more practical service to the defeated power, so far as her fleet was concerned, than victory. For while the Germans could start from scratch, her opponents, Britain in particular, started the Second War under two handicaps. The first was that her fleet, far smaller both actually and relatively than it had been in 1914, included many veteran ships, no fewer than twelve of her largest units dating from World War One. The second was that she had become overconfident that she had the measure of the submarine. She was quickly disillusioned. Within a few weeks the leading German U-boat captains had given her examples of the courage and skill of a new generation of sea officers.

Less encouraging for the Germans was the fact that again, as in 1914, her merchant fleet disappeared from the seas and oceans, except for the occasional disguised raider and blockade-runner. Moreover, in December 1939 the *Graf Spee,* which had been engaged in commerce disruption, was intercepted by a cruiser squadron in the South Atlantic. She was shadowed and damaged, and was later blown up by her own crew.

The action in which the *Graf Spee* was involved was not so much important in itself as indicative of a pattern in the sea warfare of the Second World War. This showed that the brightest of the younger commanders served with submarines, first under the direction of Admiral Dönitz and then, after 1943, of Admiral Raeder. They took a huge toll in merchant shipping, which would have been still more catastrophic but for skill in routing convoys, as well as sinking ships of war. Valuable units such as the battleship *Barham* and the aircraft carrier *Ark Royal* fell to German aces, both of them in the Mediterranean.

The part played by German surface ships was altogether less distinguished. For instance, there was an occasion in 1940 when the twenty-four year old battle-cruiser *Renown,* in rough seas and poor visibility, was encountered off Norway by the *Scharnhorst* and *Gneisenau* in company. She should have become an easy victim to superior force, but in fact she compelled the two German ships to retire, and in so doing gave an example of the fact that, in surface

The battle-cruisers *Seydlitz* (centre) and *Derflinger* (left) exercising with destroyers.

right
Admiral Scheer
(1863–1928),
Commander-in-Chief
of the High Seas Fleet in
the First World War.

below
Battleships of the High
Seas Fleet steaming to
take up their stations at
Jutland, 1916.

fighting, the British had lost none of the aggressive spirit for which they had been famous. During the following year the *Scharnhorst* and *Gneisenau* were used as raiders, but they were never prepared to face opposition in any strength, not because of any deficiencies in the ships, but by direction of the High Command. The pair made a successful dash up the Channel to their home waters, which was humiliating for the British, but the *Gneisenau* was seriously damaged by mines, which put her out of action for some time; on a later occasion, the *Scharnhorst*, attempting to attack a convoy to Russia, was intercepted and sunk, mainly as the result of the battering it received from the British battleship *Duke of York,* one of a class completed after the outbreak of war.

As for the *Bismarck* and the *Tirpitz,* for all their immense strength their active careers were brief and disappointing. In her one Atlantic sortie the *Bismarck* accounted for the veteran *Hood,* but she was herself destroyed soon afterwards. The *Tirpitz,* stationed for most of her career in Norwegian waters, held a British force

of considerable size in readiness to meet her, which would have been more valuable elsewhere. In the end she was sunk by bombs from the Royal Air Force as she lay moored near very strong shore defences. Hitler's investment in large surface ships had not paid off, and he himself was always full of criticism of the way in which they were handled.

It was among the smaller ships, not only the U-boats but also destroyers and motor gunboats, that the Germans showed themselves consistently formidable. Despite ceaseless bombing of industrial centres, the flow of production remained high, and the Germans were always capable of developing new devices such as the homing torpedo to add to the complexities of sea warfare. Above all there was the snorkel, a device which had originally been developed by Dutch technicians. This enabled a submarine to 'breathe' while underwater (except for the tip of the snorkel itself) and to retain a high speed, since diesels could be used, as when surfaced.

The snorkel-fitted Type XXI might almost be called the first true submarine, since earlier

left
Admiral Franz von Hipper (1863–1932), who led the German battle-cruisers at Jutland.

below
Battleships of the High Seas Fleet in the Skagerrak just before the Battle of Jutland, May 1916.

right
The battle-cruiser *Seydlitz* on fire after fighting at Jutland. Despite appalling damage, she survived.

below
The battle-cruiser *Derflinger*, present at Jutland, and badly damaged in the action.

Panzerkreuzer „Derflinger."

vessels were really 'diving craft', however ingenious and powerfully equipped. The XXI boats were 251 feet long, and had a surface displacement of 1,621 tons. The aim in construction was high speed under water. This was achieved, and even when forced to dive deep, very efficient electric motors gave a speed of $17\frac{1}{2}$ knots. Like many lethal weapons, they came off the production lines too late to have a decisive effect.

Another German war invention was the Walther turbine. The motive power derived from the heat energy obtained when highly concentrated hydrogen peroxide was mixed with water. The experimental prototypes gave great promise, and reached an underwater speed of 25 knots, though the cost of the fuel was astronomically high.

Having the use of the French Atlantic coastline, on which were built immense and virtually bomb-proof submarine pens, it was not perhaps so remarkable that the submarines did so much damage, as that they did not shake the morale of the British merchant crews, or win the Battle of the Atlantic outright before American help to Britain could get fully under way. After the

D-Day landings in 1944, the principal danger was over. In fact, the crucial months had occurred during the previous year. Admiral Raeder, having enjoyed an easy harvest on the far side of the Atlantic before an American convoy system could be organised, found resistance to attacks stiffening monthly and U-boat losses mounting steeply, until the balance began to tilt firmly against him.

Able as he was in the conduct of his ramified and protracted U-boat campaign, Raeder met his match in Sir Max Horton, the British Commander-in-Chief, Western Approaches, who in his younger days had been a submarine commander himself. There was also a tracking team in London Admiralty, whose top men were reputed to know what Raeder's captains were likely to do at sea better than the German Grand Admiral did himself. Such was the importance of the Atlantic struggle that it never slackened. Neither side could afford the slightest relaxation, and the intensity with which it was conducted continued until the end of the war.

The dissolution of the German fleet resulting from the Allied victory in 1945 was as complete

Destroyers and U-boats of the First World War, with a parent ship in the background.

German battleships
sailing to Scapa Flow to
surrender in 1918.

A model of the pocket battleship *Admiral Scheer*, 10,000 tons, sister ship of the *Graf Spee*. Built at Wilhelmshaven 1931–34, she carried six 11-inch guns and had a maximum speed of 26 knots. *National Maritime Museum, Greenwich.*

The pocket battleship *Graf Spee* scuttled off Mont Video, 1939, after action with a British squadron.

right
Grand Admiral Dönitz, who conducted the U-boat campaign of the Second World War.

below
The *Bismarck*, 40,000 tons and armed with eight 15-inch guns, which was sunk by a British fleet in May 1941.

as it had been after the First World War. It was marked by what was certainly one of the biggest single marine disasters of all time. A German steamer, crammed with naval and air technicians, proceeding on a westerly course in the Baltic towards the homeland on 18 February 1945 to escape from the Russians, was torpedoed by one of their submarines with the loss of 4,120 lives. She was the *Wilhelm Gustloff* of 25,484 tons.

It was the Germans who had shown the rest of the world the full implications of submarine warfare, and developed it to the limits. They now had a taste of it themselves, as a prelude to military eclipse. German sailors had fought valiantly to the last, as their soldiers had always done. It was their leaders who had sacrificed them, by a succession of decisions, tempting to those set upon aggrandisement at other people's expense, from which no nation deserved to profit.

There had been a well-known cartoon, issued during the First World War, showing the Kaiser at a lectern as if in prayer. The caption was: 'Let us prey'. He had indeed preyed, and so had Hitler. It had cost millions of lives, and the reason for ultimate failure lay in the fact that, if you prey, you may find that, given time, your victims may recover and rend you.

above
The heavy cruiser *Hipper*
in dock at Brest in the
Second World War,
with camouflage nets.

left
Grand Admiral Raeder,
Commander-in-Chief
of the German Navy in
the Second World War,
with Adolf Hitler.

THE UNITED STATES FLEET

opposite page
John Paul Jones
(1747–1792), highly
successful against the
British at sea during the
War of American
Independence (1775–83).

John Paul Jones, who ranks among the founding fathers of the navy of the United States, once wrote to his friend the Comte de Kersaint:

The rules of conduct, the maxims of action, and the tactical instincts that serve to gain small victories may always be expanded into the winning of great ones with suitable opportunity; because in human affairs the sources of success are ever to be found in the fountains of quick resolve and swift stroke; and it seems to be a law inflexible and inexorable that he who will not risk cannot win.

That was well said, and among the 'small victories' to which Paul Jones referred, a whole succession had been won by himself in British home waters at the time of the American War of Independence. Of these the best known was his action with the frigate *Serapis* off Flamborough Head in the autumn of 1779. Jones, in the *Bonhomme Richard,* defeated Captain Richard Pearson, the Englishman being afterwards knighted for saving the convoy which it had been his duty to defend. Jones remarked that if he ever met Pearson again in battle, he would make a lord of him!

Although the navy of the United States dates from Jones's era, it was several generations before the country could be said to possess a fleet. As with all democracies, successive governments were reluctant to spend money on such a form of insurance, except in times of crisis. The Americans were protected by French sea power during the original struggle for freedom. In the wars of the Napoleonic era, provision had to be made to protect merchantmen, particularly from the depredations of the pirates of the Barbary Coast. During the war of 1812 with Britain, the American navy had fought brilliantly, on the Great Lakes, and in a series of single-ship actions in the Atlantic. But the need for a fleet on a large scale had scarcely become apparent even by the time of the American Civil War. Both the Federals and the Confederates could call upon a number of miscellaneous fighting vessels, but a fleet, in the more accepted sense of the term, had gradually to be built up. The Federals were fortunate in discovering, in David Farragut, an officer who may claim rank among the foremost admirals,

limited though his opportunities were. His leadership at the victory of Mobile in 1864, and his general conduct of the blockade of the southern ports, which did so much to win the war for his side, afford good examples of his skill.

Historians usually pay much attention to the weird duel in Hampton Roads which had been fought in 1862 between the Confederate *Merrimac* and the Federal *Monitor,* as illustrating an early stage in armoured sea warfare. While it was true that the episode proved the inadequacy of wooden ships as first-line fighting units, the true interest of the event lay in the ingenuity with which the *Merrimac* was salvaged, rebuilt and used, and in the fact that although the *Monitor* had been specially designed for combat by John Ericsson, her seagoing shortcomings were such that they were a continual danger to her crew.

If general lessons could be deduced from the war, it was that most of the broad strategic principles held good, exemplified by what Captain Stephen Roskill has termed the Strength, Security and Transport elements: the Strength factor lying in the capabilities of the men-of-war employed, the Security factor in the defence of essential bases and the Transport element in the merchantmen and ancillary ships, in each of which the Federals gained and held the advantage. It also showed how far ship designers had yet to go before producing ironclads reasonably satisfactory in armament, protection, speed and stability.

An important stage in the evolution of the United States fleet may be seen in the career of Alfred Mahan, who as a young officer had taken part in the Civil War. By 1886 he had risen to be President of the Naval War College, a period which resulted in the completion and publication of his *Influence of Sea Power on History.* Although this work had a much wider impact outside his own country than in it, Mahan is one of the happy instances of a prophet who received honour from his own people. After leaving the War College post he was given command of the cruiser *Chicago,* and during the course of a commission covering the years 1893–5 he was able not only to show the United States flag

left
The obverse of a medal signalising the victory of the *Constitution* over the *Guerrière* in 1812. The ship's company was awarded $50,000 prize money for this action. *National Maritime Museum, Greenwich.*

below
The fight off Boston in 1813 between HMS *Shannon*, Captain Broke, and the U.S. frigate *Chesapeake*, which was captured, checked a series of reverses suffered by the British.

The 74-gun *Delaware* in
dry dock at Gosport,
Norfolk, Virginia.
The dock was opened in
1833.

abroad, but also to make personal acquaintance with many important people who had been impressed by his writings.

At the time of the Spanish-American war of 1898 Mahan was on the Naval War Board, responsible for strategy, and he was afterwards a delegate at the peace conference at the Hague. Even before the war had opened, he had issued *The Interest of America in Sea Power, Past and Future,* which did have some effect in political circles. The events of the war itself, during which the United States fleet, at Manila in April, and at Santiago in July, showed itself so vastly superior to that of Spain, indicated that there was a danger that easy success would lead to dangerous over-confidence, a characteristic which Americans of that period had in generous measure. Circumspection was in fact demanded, for the war had shown that, while the American fleet was adequate to deal with a thoroughly inferior navy, there were problems of supply and administration which badly needed attention, and a more modern fleet was also necessary. This was because the United States was now committed in two oceans; in the Atlantic as a result of her actions in Cuba, and in the Pacific because she had taken responsibility for the Philippines.

Such has been the later course of events that there is a certain irony in the war having taken place in the interest of Cuba. Yet it was not an act of overwhelming impulse which caused American intervention, for it was a full decade since a Cuban revolt against Spanish rule had broken out, and it had taken all the patience of Secretary of State Hamilton Fish to avert war then. When insurgency started anew in the mid-

nineties, and Spain brought in nearly 200,000 troops to suppress it, it only needed a mysterious explosion on board the United States ship *Maine* in Havana to make intervention certain.

Among those who had campaigned in Cuba was Theodore Roosevelt. This dynamic man was to succeed to the Presidency after the assassination of William McKinley in 1901. At the age of forty-three he was already the most many-sided President since Thomas Jefferson, and he was able to give a new meaning to the Monroe Doctrine by his consistent work for a strong navy through which the Doctrine could be implemented. President Monroe had stated in 1823 that, in relation to South America, any interference on the part of European powers with states which had declared their independence, and had been acknowledged as independent by the United States, would be considered an unfriendly act.

Under Theodore Roosevelt the government showed a realisation that the United States was truly a world power and would henceforward play a prominent part in world affairs. The Doctrine enunciated by Monroe so far back in the past had been merely a prophetic warning. Roosevelt exerted himself in the Far East to maintain an 'open door' for trade in China, and to prevent that country from being torn to pieces by other nations. He used the Monroe Doctrine to assume a broad responsibility for the welfare of the weaker Caribbean republics. He also took steps to bring about peace between Russia and Japan, and supported the International Court of Justice at the Hague. He did not live up to his own best principles in his attitude to Columbia, when he

wished to ensure United States dominance in Panama at the time when the construction of the strategic Atlantic-Pacific canal was in progress; but this was due to his belief that such an internationally important venture must be under the aegis of a power able to defend it in all circumstances. This was a consideration which strengthened the hand of those who saw the need for a formidable fleet.

No country was more concerned about the effects of the Japanese victory over the Russians at Tsushima than the United States. The Anglo-Japanese alliance had been looked upon with some misgiving, and strategists realised that the permanent occupation and fortification of Hawaii and Guam were essential if advanced naval bases were to be provided to safeguard American interests in the Philippines. The United States had fought a war to extirpate 'colonialism' in the Caribbean and the Pacific. It was now constrained to assume the heavy burdens from which no colonial power can hope to escape.

Theodore Roosevelt's chief naval gunnery expert, an officer who had an influence on the reshaping of the American fleet comparable with that of Sir Percy Scott in Britain, was at that time Lieutenant-Commander William S Sims. Sims had come to exactly the same conclusion as Fisher and others in Britain: it was the necessity for a one-calibre main armament, a course which was to lead to the launching of the *Dreadnought*.

Early in 1905 Congress authorised the construction of two battleships, the *Michigan* and

the *South Carolina,* whose specifications had been worked out the year before, though as the pair were not actually in commission until 1909, the *Dreadnought* had a three-year start. They mounted eight 12-inch guns, were well protected, had a speed of 18½ knots, and their lattice masts, designed for strength and range-finding ability, made them among the most distinctive ships afloat. They were the first to have their main batteries along the centre line, with super-firing guns. They were very successful fighting ships. They were important in the history of the United States fleet in that they were the first of a long succession of Dreadnought-type battleships, the last of which are still afloat, either suitably preserved in sheltered waters, or as fleet reserves.

Six other ships followed the *Michigan* and *South Carolina.* Armament was increased, and so was speed. When Britain introduced the 13·5-inch gun, America replied with the *New York* and *Texas,* laid down in 1911 and mounting 14-inch guns. There followed the *Oklahoma* and *Nevada* in which the protection of vital parts was carried to its practical limits: 18 inches on the turrets and trunks, 16 inches on the conning tower, and over 13 inches in a waterline belt and around the funnel base.

Seven more of the 14-inch type, oil fired and powered by turbines, virtually invulnerable to damage by shells where this would matter most, *i.e.* in turrets and engine rooms, all with a well-balanced profile, were built between 1914 and 1921. Constructors had their eye mainly on con-

below
American submarines of the First World War in port.

bottom
The battleship *Illinois*, 1902, one of the big ships launched immediately after the Spanish-American War.

below
Anglo-American accord in the First World War. A group on board the U.S. battleship *New York*, operational in both World Wars. Left to right: Admiral of the Fleet Lord Beatty (1871–1936); Admiral Rodman, U.S. Navy (1859–1940); King George V (1865–1936); Admiral Sims, U.S. Navy (1858–1936): the Prince of Wales, later Edward VIII and Duke of Windsor (1894–1972).

opposite, top
The U.S. battleship *Michigan*, with all-big-gun armament, commissioned in 1909 and in service during the First World War. Note the typical lattice or 'bird-cage' masts.

opposite, bottom
The U.S. battleship *Nevada* approaching Brooklyn Navy Yard. She was one of a line of 14-inch-gunned Dreadnoughts built in America between 1911 and 1921.

temporary Japanese building, as it was correctly believed that Britain would take care of the surface threat from the Germans, and that Japan would become an American responsibility. The original battleship programme was completed by a trio of 16-inch gun ships, laid down in answer to the Japanese *Mutsu* and *Nagato*. Further vessels were on the drawing board, and work had been begun on some of them, but it was halted in 1922 after the Washington Naval Conference. Two ships, the *Saratoga* and the *Lexington*, were completed as outsize aircraft carriers.

Just over a century after the ending of the war of 1812, the United States was drawn into the First World War on the side of the Western democracies. The United States fleet was by that time of such strength that it made doubly sure of victory at sea. What was infinitely valuable was the rate at which merchant ships were turned out in American yards to make good the appalling losses inflicted by unrestricted U-boat warfare.

There also began one of the most wholehearted collaborations in naval history. This was between the United States fleet and that of Great Britain. It was established in three main areas: at the base at Scapa Flow, in the Orkneys, from which the British Grand Fleet, at that time under the command of Admiral Sir David Beatty, made its sweeps; at bases in Ireland such as

Queenstown (now Cobh), from which anti-submarine warfare was conducted; and at Gibraltar, where much of the work involved convoy protection.

The United States declared war on Germany in April 1917. By November, a battle squadron under Admiral Hugh Rodman arrived at Scapa. Rodman had specifically asked that he should be given no instructions beyond his routine sailing orders. He wrote:

I realised that the British Fleet had had three years of actual warfare and knew the game from the ground floor up; that while we might know it theoretically, there would be a great deal to learn practically. There could not be two independent commanders in one force if our work was to be harmonious, and the only logical course was to amalgamate our ships and serve under the command of the British Commander-in-Chief . . . I told him if he would confide in me . . . and trust me, I would, during our stay in the Grand Fleet, adopt the same code of signals, visual and otherwise, even their secret code, which I promised never to divulge.

Admiral Rodman's account deserves quotation because just over a quarter of a century later, when the United States fleet was engaged in critical operations against Japan, this was exactly the spirit which animated the British

The U.S. battleship
Arizona blows up during
the Japanese attack on
Pearl Harbor, 7
December 1941. Behind
her are the *Tennessee*
and *West Virginia*, both
of which were damaged
in the attack.

Fleet Admiral Chester
W Nimitz,
Commander-in-Chief of
the U.S. Fleet in the war
against Japan.

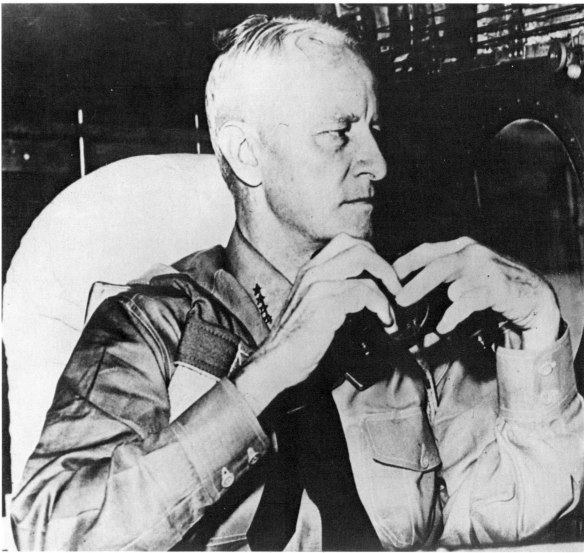

flag officers and captains who served in the same area.

From the outset the Sixth Battle Squadron, as Rodman's ships were designated, worked in complete unity with the Grand Fleet. The vessels were the *New York* (flag), *Texas, Wyoming, Arkansas, Florida* and *Delaware*. Within three days of their arrival they took part in a full-scale fleet exercise, and found no difficulty in conforming with British tactical manoeuvres, although two details caused considerable surprise. The first was the way in which accurate station keeping on winter nights was expected, with no lights showing. The British said they did it by scent! The other was the way in which the tideway of the Pentland Firth could toss great ships about like corks. It was not long before Rodman and his captains were so completely integrated that at times the American admiral would find himself senior officer, with British flag commanders under his command.

The Commander-in-Chief of the United States naval forces in European waters was Admiral Sims, who had done so much earlier in his career to improve the gunnery of his country's fleet. He was much admired in London and in December 1917, only a month after the arrival of the battle squadron, he was invited to become an honorary member of the Board of Admiralty and to share in its deliberations. The compliment was unprecedented, and although Sims was forbidden by President Wilson to take up the offer, it was appreciated none the less. It was indeed a totally different spirit than had prevailed in any earlier naval war.

In Ireland the Americans had most to do with Admiral Sir Lewis Bayly, with whom they worked in complete harmony; so much so that in Sims' words, Bayly, who was 'Uncle Lewis' to the Americans:

...always referred to his command as 'my destroyers' and 'my Americans,' and woe to any one who attempted to interfere with them or do them the slightest injustice! Admiral Bayly would fight for them against the combined forces of the whole British Navy, like a tigress for her cubs ... Relations between the young Americans and the experienced admiral became so close that they would sometimes go to him with their personal troubles; he became not only their commander, but their confidant and adviser.

One day Admiral Bayly received a signal from a United States destroyer on patrol: 'Have sunk German submarine in position lat. 51°30′N., Long. 8°10′W. Where am I?' Bayly, somewhat puzzled, sent for the senior United States officer at the time in his headquarters, and was instantly given the answer: 'Top of the class!' The reply was flashed back, to the delight of the ship's company. When Bayly went on leave during the summer of 1917, he asked Sims to take over his command. The idea had originated with Sims, who saw in it 'an imaginative gesture designed to publicize American and British cooperation, and to head off any criticism from home that American interests are being subordinated to England's'.

Admirals Sims and Rodman died before the United States had become involved in the Second World War, but there was one strong personal link between the two World Wars. In the First World War the Assistant Secretary of the United States Navy was a rising young politician called Franklin D Roosevelt. In World War Two, this same man, a well-informed expert in naval affairs, was a principal architect of victory.

Apart from the refusal of the American people to endorse President Wilson's scheme for a League of Nations, which he believed was the means by which continuing world peace could be ensured, there were other postwar difficulties which affected the United States fleet and the country in general. One of them was the reluctance of a democracy to spend money on armaments. Another was the fact that Japan gained so much by the peace treaty. Although she had played a useful part as Britain's naval ally, she had not greatly contributed to victory. Yet, by the terms of the settlement, she was given mandatory powers over an islanded area of the Pacific which took in the Mariana Group with the exception of Guam, and the Marshall and Caroline Islands, both of which lay between the United State's base at Hawaii and the Philippines.

President Wilson had protested, but he had been overruled. The result, in the words of Admiral Samuel Eliot Morison, historian of the United States Fleet in the Second World War, was that 'an impossible situation in grand strategy had been created for us . . . We were promising to defend the integrity of China and the Philippines, without anything near the military means to implement such a policy.'

An inhibiting factor in the development of the

U.S. aircraft carrier force at Ultithi, Caroline Islands, including the *Wasp, Yorktown, Hornet, Hancock* and *Ticonderoga.*

fleet was a controversy, associated with Brigadier-General William Mitchell, the great pioneer of military aviation. Mitchell contended that armies and navies, even aircraft carriers, were obsolete, and that the military future lay entirely with the land-based heavy bomber. The idea was attractive because aircraft were cheap compared with ships. Practical bombing tests conducted in 1921 resulted in the sinking of moored and unarmed naval hulks; but although they caused a stir in the newspapers they did not convince advocates of a strong navy that their efforts were a waste of time. They did, however, emphasise the increasing importance of the air factor in future war at sea. In this respect the United States was at an advantage in that her naval air arm was a purely naval responsibility and not, as in Britain, a starved section of an independent Air Force.

Already, in May 1919, Lieutenant-Commander Albert C Read of the United States Navy had made the first air crossing of the Atlantic, with a crew of four, calling at the Azores. The first nonstop flight was made in the following month from Newfoundland to Ireland by two Royal Air Force officers, Alcock and Brown. The scene seemed to be set for the development of a powerful air-sea component.

Many years earlier, in 1911, a civilian pilot, Eugene Ely, had landed a biplane on an improvised flight deck on the United States cruiser *Pennsylvania*. From then onwards progress had been steady though slow, in the United States, Britain and Japan, in all of whose fleets seaplane tenders had been commissioned. These were in

time to be phased out in favour of the aircraft carrier proper. This was to be the most important surface ship of the future, and the comparatively slow-moving squadrons of ships of the line would disappear for ever. Traditional, stately and extravagant, they were now becoming obsolete and the battleship, as a type, would continue to have value mainly as a mobile battery.

The approach of the United States to the Second World War was very different from its attitude to the First. It had then taken two full years, after the sinking of the giant liner *Lusitania* in the Irish Sea with the loss of many American lives, to bring the country from a state of indignation to active participation against Germany. In 1939 the danger to world peace was seen clearly, and rearmament in the United States was by that date well under way.

After the fall of France in 1940, President Roosevelt was able to carry his country behind him in his determination to afford Britain every aid short of war, and the exchange of fifty elderly American destroyers for facilities in British bases in the Caribbean made the attitude of the United States clear beyond doubt. American sailors assigned to the Atlantic fleet, with the duty of helping to safeguard essential convoys, exposed to some of the roughest weather known in the Seven Seas, and to attacks by U-boats, could be forgiven for wondering how near to war they were.

By March 1941 the United States and Britain had become so close that a Staff Agreement was drawn up. This stated that if the United States were to become formally involved in war, the

The *Yorktown* on fire at Midway, June 1942.

227

principal military effort would be exercised in the European theatre. The reason for this was that it was considered that Germany was a greater threat than Japan, and as she was already engaged with Great Britain she was obviously the primary target. So much controversy arose later about the competing claims of the Pacific and the western theatres of war that it is salutary to recall this agreement, which was put forward on American initiative and was honoured by her strategists. It was a far-sighted decision.

The attack on Pearl Harbor on 7 December 1941, following Hitler's invasion of Russia six months earlier, ensured that few parts of the world would be free from hostilities or from the threat of them. Ironically, some three years earlier the United States aircraft carrier *Saratoga*, during the course of a fleet exercise, had made a successful surprise sortie on the base, a hint which was not lost on the Japanese.

Admiral Yamamoto employed his main carrier force, with 423 combat aircraft and a flotilla of submarines. There was a close screen of nine destroyers and a light cruiser, and a covering force which included two battleships and two cruisers. As the Americans were taken completely unawares, the enemy were able to sink or badly damage seven battleships and three destroyers. Among them was the *Arizona*, whose remains are *in situ* to this day, together with those of 1,103 officers and men who went down with her. In that blistering attack, during which ships' companies fought back splendidly once they realised what was happening, the United States fleet lost over 2,000 killed and 710 wounded, three times its total naval losses in the First World War.

Although the Japanese assault was in every way well planned, they had sown the seeds of their own military ruin. They had aroused the anger and power of a people whose resources were incomparably greater than their own. Moreover, as the American carriers had been away from Hawaii at the time, the fleet retained undamaged the vessels which, during the course of the next few months, would halt Japanese expansion and begin the process which within four years would annihilate the Japanese navy and merchant fleet. Incidentally, five of the big ships attacked at Pearl Harbor were repaired and rebuilt to do useful service later in the war.

It would have suited Hitler far better if Japan had exerted her main strength against Russia, with whom she had recently been engaged in a ferocious though little-publicised campaign on the mainland of Asia. As it was, he made the best of things, promptly declared war on the United States, and sent submarines across the Atlantic to harry unprotected shipping on the eastern seaboard. German captains spoke of this as their happy time, as indeed it proved, until convoys could be organised and properly safeguarded.

For the United States, the defensive phase of the war was the darkest, as it is always apt to be.

But few nations have been quicker to recover, and of their armed Services, the Navy and Marines, on whom would fall most of the burden in the Pacific, were the readiest and the best trained for it. Japanese ambition was stemmed in two carrier battles in the summer of 1942, and in the autumn of that year landings were made in French North Africa, heralds of successive stages of an Allied advance on Europe's 'soft underbelly', to use Churchill's descriptive phrase. Here the astonishing spectacle was seen of the reappearance in combat formation of the *New York* and *Texas*, two veterans of the old 'Sixth Battle Squadron' of 1917–18, rebuilt and as formidable as ever.

The first of the summer battles, fought in May in the Coral Sea, was notable in two respects. It was the first time in history that action was joined when both sides possessed aircraft carriers, and it was made clear that in future naval engagements opposing surface forces might never sight one another, aircraft taking the place of long-range guns. With carriers present, other warships were relegated mainly to tasks such as radar warning, rescue work, anti-submarine screens, and the provision of anti-aircraft gunfire.

At the Coral Sea, ranges seldom narrowed to less than 160 miles, and each side lost a carrier, the Japanese the *Shoho* and the Americans their greatly loved *Lexington*, 'Lady Lex'. The battle was a victory for the Americans in that an invasion force destined for Port Moresby in New Guinea was ordered to turn back. A later effort, planned for July, was never mounted, for by that time Japan had suffered losses which ruled out all prospect of success. These occurred at the Battle of Midway, fought on the third and fourth of June 1942. So far as distances went, it followed much the same pattern as the Coral Sea. But Midway, in its long-term effects, is fit to rank among the most decisive encounters in naval history.

The Japanese had various objects in attacking Midway, an island which served as a staging point between Hawaii and their home islands. To capture or even to neutralise it would ensure greater security to the perimeter of the huge area of conquest which had been the harvest of the earlier months of the war. There was also the possibility of destroying any American task force appointed to defend the island, for in overall strength in the Pacific, Japan still had decided superiority, as she had had at the start of the war.

Admiral Nagumo was given charge of a carrier striking-force consisting of four ships which had taken part in the attack on Pearl Harbor: the *Akagi*, *Kaga*, *Hiryu* and *Soryu*. Admiral Yamamoto, the Commander-in-Chief, was at sea with his whole force, covering the operation. He was sure that, as the Americans had not yet been able to make good all the losses of the previous December, he would not only smash the Midway

The later stages of the action at Lake Erie in 1813, during the Anglo-American War. This was a victory for the Americans under Commodore Oliver Perry which gave them control of the lake. Perry's flagship, the *Lawrence*, battered and abandoned, can be seen on the right. From it he transferred to the *Niagara* and took the British, who had thought the battle won, by surprise.
In the collection of P S Winkworth, Esq.

230

below
The U.S. carrier *Hornet*,
distinguished in several
Pacific theatres of war.
By Norman Wilkinson.
*National Maritime
Museum, Greenwich.*

opposite page
top the Battle of the Coral Sea, 1942: the crew of the
damaged U.S. carrier *Lexington* abandoning ship.
The destroyer lying alongside is taking off the sick
and wounded. *centre* the moment of the subsequent
explosion aboard the *Lexington* as the fuel tanks
went up. The captain and other officers are still
aboard. *bottom* the *Lexington* that replaced the one
in the pictures above, shown here in 1944 with a
torpedo plane landing and Hellcat fighters on the
foredeck.

right
Amphibious craft landing troops at Tinian during the Second World War. Their transports are in the background.

below
A U.S. destroyer laying a smoke screen during operations off the Normandy coast in June 1944.

defences, but annihilate any opposition likely to be met with at sea.

Events were to prove him wrong. American intelligence had gathered a very fair idea of Japanese intentions, and although carrier-borne aircraft were able to deal severely with installations on Midway itself, the Japanese were unaware of and quite unprepared for the fact that the Americans had three fleet carriers at sea in the area. These were the *Yorktown,* which had been hastily patched up after battle damage, the *Enterprise* and the *Hornet.*

It was only after action against Midway had been launched that Nagumo realised the presence of Admirals Fletcher and Spruance with their powerful ships. Then within the next few hours, although the Americans suffered the loss of many aircraft and pilots in gallant strikes, the *Akagi,* flying Nagumo's flag, received lethal wounds, as did the *Kaga* and *Soryu.* Only the *Hiryu* remained operational. This was not for long. She was sunk the next day as the result of an attack pressed home by dive bombers. In her turn, however, her aircraft had done much damage to the gallant *Yorktown.* The ship survived the battle for some days, only to fall victim to a submarine.

After the main clash the Americans, wisely, did not pursue a beaten enemy, or they would have run into the main Japanese fleet. Yamamoto, unwilling to withdraw and thus 'lose face', pounded Midway from the air and sent in the cruisers *Mogami* and *Mikuma* to shell the island at long range, as a farewell gesture. The cruisers collided in trying to avoid a submarine attack, and the damaged *Mikuma* was sunk by dive bombers from the *Enterprise.* The *Mogami* somehow struggled back to Truk, with a dismal tale to tell. The predominance of the Japanese navy in the Pacific had lasted a few days short of six months. At Midway it was undermined in the space of a few hours, and by inferior numbers: although Yamamoto commanded no fewer than 162 vessels of all sorts, the American total was a mere 76, of which one third never got into the battle.

If Midway was a turning point, there was a long road ahead, both in the Pacific and elsewhere. In the Pacific there was to be the bitter, protracted and vital struggle for Guadalcanal; then the breaking of the barrier of the Bismarck Archipelago; the struggle for the control of the Aleutian, the Gilbert and the Marshall Islands. Later came the battle of Leyte Gulf and the liberation of the Philippines, all of them essential steps towards victory. Every sea mile gained was disputed, and the art of amphibious warfare was developed to a high degree of sophistication by the United States forces.

In other theatres of war, the American fleet had the powerful support of the experienced British, who had made good many of their earlier losses, but its contribution was of the essence. Sicily, Salerno, Anzio, the ever continuing battle of the Atlantic were further impressive demonstrations of naval power. And in the massive operation which was the main preliminary to victory in Europe, the assault on Normandy in June 1944 under a Supreme American Commander, General Eisenhower, their ships played a vital part, including the irrepressible *Texas,* and the *Arkansas,* which was yet another Sixth Battle Squadron survivor.

Great as was the American contribution to the war against Germany, it was in the Pacific that the country's most remarkable achievements lay. In scale, in courage, in sheer doggedness and in skill the campaigns of 1942–1945 make earlier sea warfare seem almost miniature. So, on land, did the struggle of Russia with Germany. Land mass and broad ocean were where the Second World War had most to teach the students of strategy and tactics.

Next to the President, the chief architects of American victory by sea were Admirals King and Nimitz. At the end of 1941 Earnest J King became Commander-in-Chief, United States Fleet and Naval representative on the Combined Chiefs of Staff Committee. Thorough master of his profession and intollerant of opposition, King held his post until victory had been won. Equally shrewd was the selection of Admiral Chester W Nimitz as Commander-in-Chief in the Pacific. Admiral Morison's tribute to him was well deserved.

He had the capacity to organise both a fleet and a vast war theatre, the tact to deal with sister services and Allied commands, the leadership to weld his own subordinates into a great fighting team, the courage to take necessary risks, and the wisdom to select, from a variety of intelligence and opinions, the correct strategy to defeat Japan.

Among the many other able leaders, perhaps the best known were Admiral Raymond A Spruance, who did so notably at Midway, and Admiral William F Halsey, who made his name as Commander, South Pacific at a dark moment in the campaign for Guadalcanal, and uplifted the hearts of all who served with him. Halsey had the gift, which has been given sparingly to sea officers, of projecting himself, so that he became a popular figure, as well known to the American public as any of their fighting men.

The United States fleet has started the war under grave disadvantages. Not only had it been taken by surprise, but it was also soon apparent that the Japanese were masters of night fighting, and that they possessed the best torpedo of any navy of the time. Their stern discipline was better than that of their opponents, and their naval attack aircraft were at least the equal of any then flying. With time and experience, all handicaps were overcome, and when it came to attrition, there could be only one result, so tremendous were American reserves of men and material.

The formal Japanese surrender, signed on board the United States battleship *Missouri* in Tokyo Bay on 2 September 1945, with Nimitz, Halsey, General MacArthur and Allied representatives present, was the due reward of supreme effort. Massive numbers of ships and aircraft had been employed in the final stages; eleven heavy and five light carriers, servicing over 1,200 aircraft. There had also been eight battleships, seventeen cruisers and over eighty destroyers. It was the most powerful naval force ever assembled.

To the thousands present, the great array might have seemed a far remove from Paul Jones or Nelson, from de Ruyter, Santa Cruz and the galleys of Lepanto. It was so: yet the result had been achieved by a fleet, by men trained to the highest excellence in combat. The basic requirements were in fact the same; they were for men and for skills, and both had been found.

Since that great day, the super-carrier has appeared, the huge *Forrestal* of 1955, a thousand feet long in her flight deck, and the *Enterprise* of 1960, 83,350 tons and nuclear powered. So has the Polaris submarine, her weapons untried in war. It must be the hope of every living creature, sailors included, that they will remain so.

The battleship *Alabama*, commissioned in 1942, which holds a fine record of service in the North Atlantic and Pacific during the Second World War. She is preserved at Mobile, Alabama.

U.S. battle squadron proceeding to Luzon in January 1945, preparatory to the landing of troops.

Select bibliography

This list comprises some outstanding items among scores which have proved valuable in the study of battle fleets. Many contain substantial bibliographies.

The Spanish Fleet
R C Anderson. *Oared Fighting Ships*, 1962
J de la Gravière. *La Guerre de Chypre et la Bataille de Lepanto*, 1888
F Braudel. *The Mediterranean and the Mediterranean World in the Age of Philip II*, Vol. 1, translated 1972
C F Duro. *Armada Espanola*, 9 Vols, 1877–1902
G de Artiano. *La Arquitectura Naval Espanola*, 1920
W Graham. *The Spanish Armadas*, 1972

The Elizabethan Fleet
J S Corbett. *Drake and the Tudor Navy*, 2 Vols, 1898
G J Marcus. *A Naval History of England*, Vol I, *The Formative Centuries*, 1961
M A Lewis. *The Navy of Britain*, 1948
G H Mattingly. *The Defeat of the Spanish Armada*, 1959
M A Lewis. *The Spanish Armada*, 1960

The Dutch Fleet
C R Boxer. *The Dutch Seaborne Empire 1600–1800*, 1965
C Wilson. *Profit and Power. A Study of England and the Dutch Wars*, 1957
C R Boxer (Ed.). *The Journal of Maarten H. Tromp*, 2 Vols, 1930
P J Blok. *The Life of Admiral de Ruyter*, translation by G J Renier, 1933
R G Rogers. *The Dutch in the Medway*, 1972

The Swedish Fleet
R C Anderson. *Naval Wars in the Baltic*, 1910. Reprinted 1969.

The Fleet of France
C de la Joncière and G Clerc-Rampal. *Histoire de la Marine Française*, 1934
A T Mahan. *The Influence of Sea Power upon the French Revolution and Empire*, 2 Vols, 1892
L Nicolas. *La Puissance Navale dans l'Histoire*, 1958
E Chevalier. *Histoire de la Marine Française sous la Première République*, 1886
E Desbrière. *La Campagne Maritime de 1805*, 1907, English translation 1933
J Mordal. *Twenty-Five Centuries of Sea Warfare*, 1959, English translation 1970

Nelson's Fleet
G J Marcus. *A Naval History of England*, Vol. 2, *The Age of Nelson*, 1971
A T Mahan. *A Life of Nelson: the Embodiment of the Sea Power of Great Britain*, 2 Vols, 1897
D Mathew. *The Naval Heritage*, 1944
O Warner. *Nelson's Battles*, 1965
A Bugler. *HMS Victory. Building, Restoration and Repair*, 1966

The Imperial Japanese Fleet
D Macintyre. *Sea Power in the Pacific*, 1972
A Walworth. *Black Ships off Japan*, 1941
G Sansom. *The Western World and Japan*, 1950
I H Nish. *Alliance in Decline*, 1972
M Fuchida and M Okumiya. *Midway*, 1957
M Okumiya and J. Horikoshi. *Zero*, 1957
R Inoguchi, T Nakajima and R Pineau. *The Divine Wind*, 1959
R J C Butow. *Japan's Decision to Surrender*, 1954

The British Grand Fleet
J S Corbett and H Newbolt. Naval Operations 1914–1918, 5 Vols, 1920–1931
A Marder. *From Dreadnought to Scapa Flow: the Royal Navy in the Fisher Era 1904–1919*, 5 Vols, 1961–1970
S W Roskill. *Naval Policy Between the Wars*, Vol. I, *The Period of Anglo-American Antagonism 1919–1929*, 1968
S W Roskill. *The War at Sea, 1939–1945*, 4 Vols, 1954–1961

The German High Seas Fleet
A von Tirpitz. *Memoirs*, 2 Vols, 1919
O Warner. *The Sea and the Sword: the Baltic 1630–1945*, 1965
R Scheer. *Germany's High Seas Fleet in the World War*, 1920
A Michelsen. *Der U-Bootskrieg 1914–1918*, 1925
H Bauer. *Reichsleitung und U-Bootseinsatz 1914–1918*, 1956
K Dönitz. *Memoirs*, 1959
E Raeder. *My Life*, 1960

The United States Fleet
S E Morison. *John Paul Jones*, 1959
A T Mahan. *The Influence of Sea Power upon History 1660–1783*, 1892
H and M Spront. *The Rise of American Naval Power 1776–1918*, 1939
A H Mahan. *Sea Power in its Relations to the War of 1812*, 2 Vols, 1905
R A Sims. *The Victory at Sea*, 1920
S E Morison. *The History of United States Naval Operations in World War II*, 15 Vols, 1948–1962

Acknowledgments

The lower illustration on page 87 is reproduced by gracious permission of Her Majesty the Queen.
The lower illustration on page 45 is reproduced by courtesy of the Master and Fellows of Magdalene College, Cambridge, the illustration on pages 46 and 47 by courtesy of the Worshipful Society of Apothecaries and the lower illustration on page 137 by courtesy of the Commanding Officer of HMS *Victory*.
Photographs A.C.L. Brussels 18 left; Bavaria Verlag–Friedrich Rauch 193; Osvaldo Böhm, Venice 11 bottom; British Museum, London endpapers, 40 bottom, 126 top; J E Bulloz, Paris 104 top left, 104 bottom, 111 top, 138–139; Bundesarchiv-Militärarchiv, Freiburg 196 top; Chicago Historical Society 229 bottom; Chief of Naval Operations–Photos in the National Archives, Washington D.C. 225 top left, 225 top right; Mary Evans Picture Library, London 108 top, 159 top; Photographie Giraudon, Paris 97, 104 top right, 108–109, 113 top, 114–115; Photographie Hachette, Paris 160; Hamlyn Group–Hawkley Studio Associates 26–27, 34, 46–47, 62 bottom, 137 top left, 178–179, 194, 195 left, 195 centre; Hamlyn Group–J A Hewes 137 bottom; Hamlyn Group–Edward Leigh 45 bottom; Hamlyn Group Picture Library 140 top, 229 top; *Illustrated London News* 180 bottom; Imperial War Museum, London 77 top, 77 bottom 118–119 bottom, 119 top, 149 bottom, 152 top, 152 bottom, 153, 155 tops, 161 top, 162 top, 162–163, 164–165, 168 right, 173 top, 174 top, 174 bottom, 177 top, 181, 182 bottom, 185 top, 188, 189 top, 189 bottom, 200 bottom, 208–209 bottom, 210 bottom, 211 top, 220 bottom, 221 bottom, 223 top, 223 bottom, 224 top, 226, 227, 233 bottom, 234 bottom, 236–237, 237 top; Kyodo Photo Service, Tokyo 147 top, 156 top, 163 top, 165 top; Larousse, Paris 98; Mansell Collection, London 145, 148, 151 top, 158–159, 167, 169 top, 172, 173 bottom, 184 bottom, 185 bottom, 187 bottom, 204 top, 213, 222; Mariners Museum, Newport News, Virginia 216–217; Maritiem Museum 'Prins Hendrik', Rotterdam 63; Mas, Barcelona 6, 9, 11 top, 14, 16 bottom, 22 top, 24 top, 25, 29 top, 30 top, 30–31, 31 top left, 31 top right; Paul Mellon Centre for Studies in British Art, London 125 top; Paul Mellon Collection, Washington D.C. 142–143; Montagu Motor Museum, Beaulieu 136 top; Musée de la Marine, Paris 100, 105 top, 106 top, 106 bottom, 110 bottom left, 110 bottom right, 112 top, 112 bottom, 114 top, 116 top, 116–117, 117 top, 118–119 centre; Museo Maritimo, Barcelona 29 bottom; Nationalhistoriske Museum paa Frederiksborg Slot, Hillerød 132 bottom; National Maritime Museum, Greenwich 2–3, 10, 12–13, 15, 16 top, 17 left, 17 right, 18–19, 22 bottom, 23 bottom, 24 bottom, 28 top, 28 bottom, 33, 36, 37, 38–39, 39 right, 40 top, 41, 43, 44 top left, 44 top right, 48 top, 48 bottom, 50–51, 51 top, 51 bottom right, 52, 53 top, 53 bottom, 56 top, 56–57, 58–59, 59 right, 60–61 top, 60–61 bottom, 66–67, 68, 69, 70–71, 74 top, 74 bottom, 75 top right, 75 bottom, 76 top, 76 bottom, 86 top left, 89 top, 89 centre, 105 bottom, 107, 121, 122 top left, 123, 125 bottom, 126–127, 128 top, 128 bottom, 129 top, 129 bottom, 130–131, 132 top, 134–135, 136 bottom, 142 top, 164 top, 176, 177 bottom, 186, 187 top, 195 right, 208–209 top, 214–215, 215 top, 218, 232; Nationalmuseum, Stockholm 86 top right, 88 top, 90–91, 101 bottom, 102–103; National Portrait Gallery, London 45 top left, 45 top right, 122 top right, 124 top, 127 top, 143 right; Navy Department–Photos in the National Archives, Washington D.C. 161 bottom, 225 bottom; Nederlandsch Historisch Scheepvaart Museum, Amsterdam 23 top, 62 top, 64, 65 top, 75 top left; Nordisk Pressefoto, Copenhagen 101 top; Parker Gallery, London 124 bottom, 214 bottom, 215 bottom; Popperfotos, London 154–155, 156 bottom, 221 top, 224 bottom, 233 top, 233 centre; Radio Times Hulton Picture Library, London 149 top, 150, 151 bottom, 168 left, 170–171 top, 220 top; La Réunion des Musées Nationaux, Paris 99, 109 top, 113 bottom; Rijksmuseum, Amsterdam 20–21, 55, 65 bottom, 72 top, 72 bottom, 73 top, 73 bottom, 84–85; Franklin D Roosevelt Library, Hyde Park, New York 147 bottom, 157 top; Royal Naval Museum, Portsmouth 81, 137 top right; 140 bottom; Science Museum, London 42, 44 bottom, 49, 169 bottom, 170–171 bottom, 182–183, 184 top, 190–191; Bradley Smith, New York 157 bottom; Staatsbibliothek Preussischer Kulturbesitz, Berlin 79, 179 top, 180 top, 196 bottom, 203 top; Statens Sjöhistoriska Museum, Wasavarvet, Stockholm 80 top right, 80 bottom, 82, 83, 86 bottom, 87 top, 90–91 bottom, 92 top, 92 bottom, 93 top, 93 bottom, 94 top, 94 bottom, 95 top, 95 bottom; Stockholms Stadsmuseum 88–89; Süddeutscher Verlag, Munich 197, 199 top, 201, 202 top, 202 bottom, 203 bottom, 206–207, 210 top, 211 bottom; Tate Gallery, London 35; Ullstein Bilderdienst, Berlin 198, 199 bottom, 200 top, 204 bottom, 205; United States Bureau of Ships–Photo in the National Archives, Washington D.C. 219; United States Coast Guard–Photo in the National Archives, Washington D.C. 234–235; United States Naval Academy Museum, Annapolis, Maryland 111 bottom; Weidenfeld and Nicolson, London 230–231.

Index

Figures in italics refer to illustrations

239